The Heart

ANNA J. SMITH

authorHOUSE°

AuthorHouse™
1663 Liberty Drive
Bloomington, IN 47403
www.authorhouse.com
Phone: 1 (800) 839-8640

Published by AuthorHouse 07/27/2018

ISBN: 978-1-5462-5330-3 (sc)
ISBN: 978-1-5462-5329-7 (e)

Dedication

I would like to thank my Granddaughter for her help with ideals for the book. And for giving me the courage to put my mother's words into print so all could enjoy.

THE HEART

How much pain
Can the human heart stand?
How strong was it made,
When life first began?
Does it stand as much happiness?
Does anyone know?
Thru joy or pain,
Is the beat fast or slow?
How nice that the heart,
Isn't on the outside,
There's feelings sometimes,
That we'd like to hide.
How nice that our face,
Doesn't let our heart down,
As we go around,
With the face of a clown.
It's quite a large heart,
With plenty of space,
To hold all emotions,
As thru life we race.
It won't burst with happiness,
Or break with pain,
As a broken heart, Folks,
Would not beat again.

1960

SILENT TEARS

Your face is laughing.
Light and gay.
Your eyes are deep and
Sad today.
I see a tear, well
In your eye,
But past your eye-lid,
Doesn't slide.
Where did it come from,
Dearest one?
Back of the brain,
Way out of the sun?
The sun of love
That's set, won't rise?
Is that what makes, your
Eyes to cry?
No matter what you,
Try to do,
These silent tears, still
Follow you.
They're memories, that
Hurt within,
That's why in tears, you
Also grin.

1960

TOMMY

"Oh! Tommy, you fell in your pants",
Said Mother, with a gasp.
"I couldn't take them off," said Tom,
"Because I fell too fast".

Tommy cried, to go to school,
Right up to age of five,
And now he won't,
Climb on the bus,
Unless I tan his hide.

GRAMP

Tired Grandpa wished, for years to pass,
So he could then retire,
But now he's up, at crack of dawn,
With energy and fire.

1960

SWEET NOTHING - SHARON

This weekend coming,
There's a super Ball.
Gosh! what a dream guy,
This Ray so tall.
All the girls like him,
They think he's just swell.
He likes me, I know,
Way he smiles, that tells!
There's a lovely gown,
Down at the store.
I'll look like a Queen,
Then he'll date me more.
I know Mom will say,
"Yes, you may go".
Dad has to be sure,
The guy is just so.
"Small, Red Rose Corsage",
I'll tell him to bring.
"Oh! my heart will pound,
When the door bell rings".
We will rock and roll,
And he'll serve me punch.
Maybe afterwards,
We'll stop for a lunch.
She flopped on her back,

Upon her twin bed.
With gay fancy dreams,
Floating 'round in her head.
In her rich day dreams,
Everything was all set.
Except dream guy Ray,
Hadn't asked her yet.

1960

RENTED CAMP

The truck was loaded,- boxes and kids,
We headed for camp, like the others did.
Bumped over the road, Momat the wheel.
We dreamed of the lake, how it would feel.

The landlord met us, held out the keys.
We gave him a check, his eyes looked pleased.
We jumped around, unloaded the truck,
Getting out of work, we'd always duck.

We'd keep late hours, each morning we'd sleep.
As the sun got high, from the sheets we'd peep.
Swam in the warm lake, fished from the dock,
Went barefoot all day, no more dirty socks.

Rowed the boat 'cross, the lake so wide,
To visit some friends, see their camp inside,
Floated on tire tubes, jumped from their raft,
Acted crazy, you'd think we were da ft.

Mom and Fay in the old camp chairs,
While getting brown, lost the oil from their hair.
But than who cares, 'bout those little things,
Not them - not now - just pure re-lax-ing.

Soon, company came - company went,
Some stayed all night, on chaise lounges unbent.
Had hot pizza, beer, soda and chips
Lopped down so much, got broad thru the hips.

The week was so short - the days just flew,
Hated to leave, many things to do,
Packed up our boxes - loaded the truck,
So back to the farm. Next year? With luck!

July 23, 1960

WHO CAN?

Can man make a flower?
Make a humming bird wing?
Manufacture a stately old tree?

Can man make a seed?
A cow that gives milk?
The water we use, for our needs?

Can man make the grass?
The birds in the air?
Make the fruit, that hangs on a tree?

Can man make a sun?
Make a moon like above?
Make an earth, which grows all our feed?

So remember my children,
We need the good Lord,
Count the Blessings around you, you see,

Because once,
THE LORD,
Made all of these.

PESKY FLY

A fly flew in the open door,
O Boy! a new place, to explore!
Lit on the table, sink and chair,
Next upon the Wifey's hair.
He should have left her right alone,
For now, "His life will end", she moaned.
Kids laughed, to see the merry chase,
Of fly and wife around the place.
She swatted at the fleeing fly,
And yelled, "Oh! yes, your going to die".
The fly soon stopped, spied some friends,
The wifey swung, his life to end.
Raised the swatter, looked underneath,
Gave a gasp, then started to beef,
The flies were, lined-up for Masses,
But there laid, her only eye glasses.

1960

I WISH

I wish I were fly paper,
And you a tiny fly,
Then I could hold you tightly.
From me you'd never fly.

I wish I were an auto,
And you the roads I use,
For I could follow, you then,
Be with you as I choose.

I wish I were the raindrop,
And you the earth below,
Then I could kiss you often,
Instead of dreaming so.

The times you made me angry,
With stupid things you said,
I wish you were, some large nail,
And I a hammer head.

EARLY A.M.

The alarm goes off,
The house does stir,
The beds do creak,
Dog shakes his fur.
Start the breakfast,
Oh! Mother dear,
For soon you'll have
Some voices near.
"Mom, did you iron
My good pink blouse".
"I can't find anything
in this house".
"See if my bra
Is on the chair?"
Please will you throw
It up the stairs".
"Who's in the bathroom?
Let me in".
"There's not much time,
You can't shave, Tom".
Over the din,
Mom loudly shouts,
"You'll miss the bus,
I have no doubt".

Breakfast eaten,
Lunches in hand,
Out by the road,
Laughing they stand.
Wearing their clothes
Grudgingly shared,
"Yes, they made it
With time to spare".

1960

FRIENDLY TELEPHONE

Baby likes the telephone,
He plays with it,
All day at home.
The bell rings,
He's the first one there,
Sure gets in his sister's hair.
The phone rings, a lot,
For them after school.
Five minutes to talk,
Would be a good rule.
They see each other,
In school everyday,
I wonder there's anything
Left to say.
The telephone, is
a very nice thing,
It brings surprises,
Each time it rings.
The baby enjoys it,
The teenagers too,
Pa pays the bill,
What else can he do?

1960

HEART - BREAK HILL

Lonely, night and day,
Groping, lost the way.
Path was different,
On which I trod.
I was tired,
But onward, I plod.
Hard going up-hill,
Moaning,
Met sad folks,
All were groaning.
They wouldn't stop,
Or show me the way.
Had their own troubles,
"Sorry," they'd say.
Disgusted, stumbling along,
Tear-filled eyes, mind without song.
Footsteps echo, along
The wrong path,
Each hump in the road,
Hoped was my last.
Weary, weak, stone sat upon,
Not caring, wouldn't go on.

A hand fell on,
My sobbing bent head,
"I'll show you the way,"
A soft voice said.
Hands clasped,
Lighter the feet,
Strolling on, breathing deep.
Shadows of lonesomeness,
Left behind,
As once more, Love
Began to shine.
Well traveled, Heart-Break Hill,
Brief, hard, traveled still.
Always,
There's someone,
Who'll walk with you.
The Hill is known,
The path isn't new.

Bob, a boy with freckles,
Spent summer days with me,
Every day went swimming,
'Twas in the creek, you see,
Farm was fun, sun was hot,
Outdoors he stayed the most,
Soon the sun did change him,
Into a sore PINK GHOST.

GREEN EYES

Green Eyes, such a pretty hue.
Should be on me, instead of you.
The prettiest I've ever seen,
Do they shoot sparks, when you feel mean?
Brows so dark, eye lashes, so.
Do boys love them, I'd like to know?
Do they follow you around,
'Till Papa wears a mean old frown,
Better scatter boys!
Papa makes a lot of noise.

YOUNG FARM LAD

My Daddy has a big busy, fun farm.
With a lot of cows, locked up in his barn.
The little calves, all rope-tied in their place.
I love to pat them and rub their face.
Every morning, just before six o'clock,
My Daddy puts on his big boots and socks,
Climbs into his jacket, grabs his barn hat.
Gone to milk cows, I do love to watch that.
When I grow up and become a big boy,
I'll be a farmer, the farm I enjoy.
Drive the big tractor, "Boy! What a honey!"
Of course when I work, I Should Get Money!"

WORKING WIFE

She left the house early,
Went looking for work.
Wondering, how could she
Have married this jerk.
Was tired of his wallet,
So damn awful flat.
It helped her decide,
She did not come back.

CHICK

Yellow, soft, small to hold,
You'll lay eggs, someday I'm told,
You feel so nice against my face,
You eat your mash, just love the taste.

Wait for it to lay an egg,
But do not hold your breath I beg,
Or you will find it pretty rough,
Twill be a rooster sure enough.

Sure they love the mash but honey,
That stuff cost a lot of money,
And when he grows into a rooster,
He won't be cute then like he use to,
He does a lot of messing too,
And that stuffs' nasty on your shoe.

DONKEY

Donkey, donkey in the road,
You can carry heavy loads,
Pull a cart, with children in it,
And get stubborn any minute.

1960

HOME

Babies cry,
Husbands moan,
Doors get slammed,
Tapes a-spin,
Shuffling bones,
If things were quiet,
You'd know, you weren't home.

CHILD'S SNOWFLAKES

Dancing softly from the sky,
On my hat, into my eye,
Passed my nose, upon my boot,
Even clings to my snowsuit,
Just like God's, White Angels,
In a story, Mother tells.
Gliding gently to the ground,
Never hear you make a sound.

GROWING PAINS

He ran 'cross the lawn.
Feet flew up the steps.
Forgot that his leg,
Had been sore.
Jump over a chair,
Flopped down on the couch.
Turned his radio up,
To a roar.
Must save his money.
Must learn, how to dance.
"I've had my last crewcut, no more!"
How happy was he
It would be his first date,
With the lovely young lady, next door.

INTERUPTED

Two lovers sat down, in the old porch swing,
Bright moon-light night, you could see everything.
He put his arm, across her back,
Gave her a squeeze, and a friendly pat.
Was just going to kiss, her golden hair,
But father appeared, and was standing there.
How'd Pa know, they were in the swing?
They'd forgotten to oil, the gosh darn thing.

1960

BOY ON A BEACH

I sat on the Beach,
With a roving eye.
Out on the high dive,
A girl I did spy.
Could dive like an eagle,
With Movements just so.
Swims strong and smooth,
This girl I must know.
I hung 'round the beach,
Getting brick-red.
Must meet her, right now,
Her form, went to my head.
She walked up the beach,
Dripping wet,
I felt so foolish,
It was my sister Claudette.

1960

SCHOOL BLUES FLY

Summer gone, School begins,
New clothes for school, must buy,
Hair needs shears and new curl,
There's just, one reason why!

Picnics are all over,
On beaches you can't lie,
Bedtime must be early,
Each night all week, Oh! My!

Thoughts, of all the school fun.
New kids who'd catch your eye,
Ball games, sock hops, parties,
These thoughts makes, school blues fly.

Speaking, laughing, fooling,
New classmates amble by,
Got an introduction,
New slick chicks, real cool guys.

TEDDY PLAYS

I can climb a tree,
I can catch a Bee,
I can jump and run,
I have lots of fun.
I have a dog, that likes to bark,
But never speaks, when I say, "Hark".

I can ride a bike,
I can go on hikes,
I like to catch fish,
While I sit and wish,
I'm a busy lad, as you can see,
Come on along, and play with me.

BUY ME A FRIEND

I'd like someone to play with me.
Each day I play alone.
Or follow Mom and Dan around,
Our farm, the barn, my home.
My three sisters are much older,
I only bother them,
They have their own school friends, you see,
So I'm without a friend.
I asked my Dad, "Buy me a Friend".
A puppy would be right,
For he would always play with me,
Be with me day and night.
I don't want a soft white kitten,
For they are just for girls,
Small Billy Goat might fit real fine,
Or tiny bouncy squirrels.
Big Porky Pig, muddy and mean,
Must keep him in a pen.
The Rabbit with the wiggly nose,
Could almost be a friend.
A monkey could stay in a cage,
But Mom would say, "No, No",
If he were loose around the house,
He'd surely have to go.

My books upon the shelf are swell,
For Mommy reads to me,
I dream that I am in there, too,
Just busy as can be.
Old toys stuffed in the corner box,
Give hours of good fun,
Just building homes, play with my cars,
Or watch my train to run.
But animals aren't what I want,
Or books upon my shelf,
I'd like to buy a real live boy,
The same size, as my self.

1960

CHILD HIDDING

Tiny brown tree toad,
He lives in the trees,
Sometimes stays hidden,
They're real hard to see.

Turtle lumbering,
Feet scrape cross the road,
A green warty frog,
He croaks, way down low.

Brown, fat Mr. Woodchuck,
Alert by his hole,
Colored fish splash,
In a brook that's cold.

Nervous, Mom Partridge,
Flutters in thicket,
Concealing her nest,
With babies in it.

Foxes play around,
Their underground den,
If they once spied me,
All my fun would end.

Hid in the Meadow,
Stayed part of a day,
To watch and listen,
What nature would say.

MY LITTLE GIRL

Light-hearted Jean, age of nine,
Plays with her friends, all day, just fine.
She likes the girls, mostly the boys,
They seem to be her greater joys.

She likes to sing and dance and play,
And go visiting, if she may.
Just like a frog, all full of hops,
She's really tired, before she stops.

TED'S BLUE COVERALLS

My Daddy came home,
From downtown shopping,
Had a brown package,
And gave it to me.
I tore it wide open,
And smiled with joy.
Bib Overalls,
Like Dad's were, you see.

I put them on quickly,
Then strolled about,
Hands in my pocket,
Oh! they fit just right.
"I'll wear them all day".
I said to my Dad.
Mom said, "You do,
Make a manly sight".

So many pockets,
To rill with good things,
I'll get some of Dad's,
Old greasy small tools.
I'll carry some gum,
And a watch and pad,
A hammer and nail,
Bright wrench and shipped rule.

I can borrow Dad's,
Old not-used wallet,
My Mom will give me,
A pencil to use.
Gosh! even yet there's
More pockets to fill,
I have nothing left,
Now, that I can use.

I have a pocket,
Up here in my Bib,
It's roomy enough,
For my friendly Frog.
The long middle slit,
Will give him fresh air,
Then he'll stay healthy,
As when in the bog.

I've two front pockets,
Left empty, it seems,
So I can use them,
To stick in my hands.
Or carry my stones,
New pennies and string,
So I won't lose them,
Again in the sand.

I like this present,
I opened today,
Helps me be busy,
As ever I can,
I'll go with my Dad,
Be busy all day,
"By Golly, Gee Whiz!
I'm like a big man".

ED'S 75ᵀᴴ PARTY

There was a good man in this town.
At home could never be found,
His truck on the road,
School Bus he drove,
Or Legion Hall having a round.

The school kids did so like this guy,
"Your rules sure are tough", they would sigh.
But did what he said,
And kept a cool head,
Their respect for Ed was high.

Always ready to help neighbors out,
His best work was never in doubt,
His face had a grin,
Friendly words did ring,
When Ed was out round about.

So, Ed, be proud of your life,
And "Thank God," you have a good wife,
Enjoy, your "Big" Party.
Eat, very hearty,
And blow out, the candles just right.

WHO?

He said he would write,
And I know he will,
But I can't remember,
If it was John or Bill.

He said he would mail it,
Right after he called,
But I can't remember,
Who said it, at all.

Now I must suffer,
And now I must wait,
I hope he remembered,
And the letter's not late.

I'm really quite lucky,
With my memory, so bad,
I'll think, I've got boyfriends,
Also, more than I have.

MAYBE?

Shaken,
I ponder the words,
"Maybe tomorrow".
Words tossed out,
As I closed the car door,
After I asked,
"When will I see you again?"

Will we be as close then,
As we were tonight?
Maybe!
How can I know, that there,
Will be one more extra day?

GRAM (TO THE LITTLE FOLK)

I go by different names, from my two and three year olds. To one I'm "Mom-mac", another "Grandma Butts", and another Mrs. Butter.

Smiling they bounce along the old cracked sidewalk. Only to inevitably, push their little fingers against the low hung button door bell.

Animal books piled under the T.V. stand, are removed. A little hand drags, me in tow, to lie on the floor and spend hours flipping pages over again and again.

I must watch the amazing feat, of how good one can jump, from the back of the sofa, down.

I have learned about "Magic Garden". Playing it, entails, hiding in the closet and singing "Magic Garden", only after we let in Tom and Jerry our friends.

I learned about "Fraggle Rock". To Mommy's exercise record, danced the game of "Ring-a-around-the-Rosy".

On nice days, it's always fun to walk around the street block, pulling a wagon empty. They couldn't understand, why they couldn't sit upon other people's front steps.

We ride around the house, in an old wheel-barrow. Play ball, then climb onto the donkey-planter and ride to no-where.

The time goes fast and at the end, I settle into my soft rocking chair, and realize, youth can keep on going forever.

FATHER'S REPLY

"So you want to marry,
My daughter, my lad?"
The father grinned,
Oh, yes! he was glad.

He looked at the boy,
And shook his head.
The lad stood there,
His face getting red.

"You know what you're doing?
All thought out clear?
Got a good job,
The rest of the year?"

"You must find a home!
Buy you a car!
You know your money,
Won't go very far!"

"I'm not trying,
To scare you, laddy, my boy,
But making a living,
Isn't all joy".

"Yes, I know, you're in love,
And see eye to eye,
But will it last,
In the great bye and bye?"

"I've not lost a daughter,
I've gained a son,
You've lost your freedom,
Your life's just begun".

"Work is your by-word.
Money a must.
Making a future,
By Golly! Or Bust!"

"I can relax,
And rock in my chair,
I've been there, my son,
But who in hell cares".

HOSPITAL STAY

There was an old man, on a Hill.
His knee wouldn't work, as he willed.
He went to see Doc,
Cause his knee would lock,
Sad, he's now in, a Hospital.

The nurse made him march, off to bed.
She sponged off his flushed, fevered head.
He was quite mental,
Temps they were rectal.
"Quit moving, lie still", the Nurse said.

He grumbled as he passed his time.
An idea soon, came to mind.
He giggled with glee,
What fun there would be.
He was high, so high, like on wine.

He'd play that he was, in "Roma".
Wait for the fat Nurse, "Leona".
He would pinch her buns,
The "son-of-a-gun",
He did, got knocked, in a coma.

The bed pans, were cold, from the start.
To lie there in bed, broke his heart.
He tried to be good,
And act like he should,
But his "Johnny" kept, coming apart.

"Keep your chin up, Smitty, my boy".
And wait for those days filled with Joy.
Golfing or bowling,
Just simply strolling.
Won't be long, you can play, with your toys.

JUST PARENTS

Being Father and Mother,
Takes all of your time,
Years deep in sorrow,
Years dipped in sunshine.
Both worry and gladness,
Rides the same days,
Future is cloudless,
Soon a quick haze,
No time limit set,
On raising a child,
As long as you live,
You'll walk the miles.
Begin with the baby,
Teens, married years,
You help and advise,
Be disgusted, spill tears.
You throw up your hands,
Exclaim, "I'm through",
But way down deep,
You know it's not true.
Proud to be helping,
In sunshine and sorrow,
And called, "JUST PARENTS",
Today and Tomorrow.

HECKLES

It's little things that aggravate,
Along life's winding way,
Exasperate you, till you shout,
The things you shouldn't say.
You amble to the telephone,
You have a party line,
As usual, it's busy,
They've used up all your time.
You climb into the bath tub,
For a relaxing soak,
Your eye falls on the soap-dish,
There isn't any soap.
Shampoo your hair,
Quite late at night,
Find set-pin dish in minutes,
But my daughters,
Pin-curled theirs,
And left two bent ones in it.
You start to do the dishes,
The baby screams, my soul!
You find him something else to do,
By then your water's cold.

You say I'll have a cigarette,
My nerves to quiet down,
You look and poke,
Just scrape the place,
Not one butt can be found.
Now I wonder, even more,
In my small, private dome,
If all the mothers,
Shout like me,
Sometimes within their homes.

HOLIDAYS

"Holidays", those fun words,
With their magical sound,
Create visions of joys,
As your head spins around.

Each age dreams, their own dreams,
Joyful scenes come alive,
Floating backward thru time,
Meeting days long gone by.

The young dream of "swell" fun,
They will have out of doors,
The days will be happy,
How their visions do soar.

Teenagers envision,
Time off with their friends,
Walks, shopping, just talking,
Tapes to spin, clothes to lend.

Parents dream of bustle,
Like the house to be cleaned,
How many will visit?
Not much time, so it seems.

Gram and Gramp will decide,
To visit the kids,
Spending time at each house,
Like as they, always did.

The homes "throb" and will "swell",
With laughter, Rock songs,
The days will pass quickly,
As time hurries along.

What of the lonely folks,
Who's kids moved away,
Or one partners not there,
Left this world, one sad day.

Or the woman who had,
Lots of good friends around,
She out-lived them all,
Her house empty of sound.

Holidays are sad days,
For these lonely few,
They <u>have</u> merry visions,
Of days that they knew.

But they make no new plans,
And they make, no big dreams,
It's not very much fun,
If you're alone, it seems.

Remembrance of days,
Is no fun to recall,
If unable to tell it,
So a friend, can hear all.

Holidays and Visions,
Must be cozily shared,
With whom ever you like,
Or with someone who cares.

FULL CIRCLE

What happened in those "1940 to 60" years?
When the pay was good and factories hummed,
And World War II, brought us many a tear,
Our future looked bright, and we lived on the run.

We bought or built, our very own homes,
Taught our kids old morals, and lived by the rules,
We took them to places, we'd never been,
And took them to church and Sunday School.

But somewhere, their living begin to change,
Their lives became hectic, they couldn't cope,
Our kids became selfish, became the "Big I",
Their marriages ran, like a day-time soap.

If a marriage lasted, up to fifteen years,
It would very soon wobble, shake and end,
With a hurt trip to court, and a small settlement,
And children were left, with so many loose ends.

Parent guilt rides heavy, after divorce,
They grant each wish, of the kids, so dear,
Hoping kids won't hate them, or want to leave home,
"Not-my-kid" parents, plays "Santa" all year.

What went so wrong, made their life decay?
Was it Vietnam or Korean War days?
Or was it street drugs, that hit the scene,
Making them restless, with their mind in a haze?

Did they crave love, sung of in songs,
As they played "Swap-partners", that old Social game?
Thought the grass was greener, across the fence,
But upon crossing the stile, they found no new change.

Two sets of Parents, for the children today,
Six caring Grands, step-sisters and brothers,
When it suits their fancies, a choice of two homes,
Playing mothers and fathers, against one another.

I now see my Grand-kids, become the "Big I",
Their minds mixed up, emotions out of control,
With everyone doing, his "I will" thing,
No one is settled, their so restless and bold.

I feel sorry, for all the ones who get hurt,
I can't give advice, I don't know how they feel,
So I'll pray, that they'll leave this Fantasy-Land,
And shoulder the cares, of a world that is real.

PONDERING

I sit in my chair, my legs 'cross the arm,
My roving eye spies, the Bible of mine,
Now here is a book, that gives me great thought,
Wrote by The Prophets, 'way back in time.

The "Book" is so full, of all kinds of facts,
History is told, Parables, and Rhyme,
Some people say, "I just don't understand",
They could, if they tried to relax their mind.

People say, "God does, some ugly mean things".
"God" doesn't want Blood, Revenge or be Cruel,
"He" wants what is "His", and that's just your Soul,
"He" gave you a Brain. Don't think like a fool.

Men become Preachers and says "God called them",
How come they all have, the old "silver tongue"?
Does "God" really call, one man here, one there?
I'd "call" a street gang, save many, so young.

I read and think and question a lot,
And wonder if "God" and the Prophets talked?
Did Prophets say so, for it gave them control?
Did "God" say those words, as we have been told.

How come today there's no Prophets so wise,
That speaks with our God, or God speaks with them,
Do people know, who the False Prophets are?
Do we really know, who are the right men.

My "God" came as Jesus, walked on this earth,
Tender and caring, for all types of man,
"He" spoke Love, lived Love, had Love in his Heart,
"He" was "God" and "King" - for he said, "I AM".

Feb. 5, 1985

GOSSIP

Why do some people, talk about,
Someone who's been thru Hell?
Not one soul is safe from Gossip,
Town, Village, Country, Dell.

How they so delight in showing,
How other's lives are stained.
Do they think it makes them Wiser?
With gossip that brings pain?

Seems their brain is small and empty,
It's all they know to say.
Or does someone else's troubles,
Make theirs look small today?

Like things that happened years ago,
Are washed and kept like new.
By Spite and Spit upon the tongue,
Of a Boring, PEA-BRAIN few.

They never think of wondrous things,
Or read good books to grow.
They think they're clever, as they are,
With MITE-SIZE Lore they know.

The BEDROOM gossip is the best.
Who did have SEX, with who?
But! in that bedroom when it's done.
Is not you three, but two

For no one's perfect in this world.
Just human as can be.
Our "Genes", are really what we are.
We're different you and me.

My skeleton in the closet,
Won't be the same as yours.
Mistakes are made by everyone.
Life's hurts - life's open sores.

Remember when you wag your tongue,
You're not so "VIRGIN PURE".
For as you pick my bones apart,
Your skeletons a Lure.

So "LIKE" a person for "HIMSELF",
His faults will never end.
What happens in his private life,
Is not your, "DAMN" business, FRIEND.

BEATINGS OF THE HEART

The eyes of the soul,
Creep silently across her face,
Beneath the laughter,
Of today,
As a cloud passes over the sun.
Bringing anxiety and sadness,
To the blue pools,
Staring out of the face,
Of one who remembers
Yesterday.

Like a screen door,
Banging open on its hinge,
Leaving the house open,
Yet still huddled against the grass,
Her body remains huddled on the chair,
Devoid of today's scenes,
As thoughts fly swiftly away,
Of one who remembers
Yesterday.

As a feather-trigger
Sends a missle straight for home.
Words, deeds, tunes
Send her thoughts flowing,
Over the sands of time.
Weighing her down in dunes,
Of memories.
Slowing her body so still,
Death passes,
Thinking he has been here,
And touched the heart,
Of one who remembers
Yesterday.

The Angel of Darkness,
Springs the latch,
Of Pandora's Box.
The mist carries the scenes,
Around the moon-lit room.
Causing sleep to scurry
To a darkened corner,
Till it can creep silently,
Over the tear-filled eyes,
Of one who remembers,
Yesterday.

The Morning sun kisses awake,
The troubled yet fresh,
Shining eyes of blue.
They hold each others
Rays of light caresseingly
Giving the day new meaning.
By lifting the heart-beat,
To meet a gayly - dressed,
Day of everlasting happiness,
Veiled in a new-found rich love.
Drowneding the sad memories,
Of one who remembers
Yesterday.

1983

SCHOOL "BUS 67"
And School Crossing Guard

There is a Bus Driver, named Jones.
I don't think, that she's really all there.
She does some strange things,
Most days on the Bus,
And acts like, her Bat-Belfrey is bare.

She wears the boys hats, all turned a'round,
As she is driving the Bus down the road.
The Girls cute stuff toys,
On the Dashboard lay.
Teddy bears, Cats, white Rabbits and Toads.

She holds them up, just to make them dance.
One after the other, 'till she's done.
She wants you to know,
She thinks she's a clown.
So you smile, wave and nod, like its fun.

She holds down two jobs, most every day.
She sure can't be, to empty, upstairs.
Or is it because,
Her brain gets too tired,
And needs, just to get out in the air.

Whether tired or dumb, I'm glad she drives.
The kids sure like, her gay happy soul,
With her shinny eyes,
Her bright smiling face,
And she makes me feel warm, when I'm cold.

I stand on my corner, every day.
Knowing that soon, her Bus will appear.
Just whipping along,
Like she owns the road,
With her Bus full of sunshine and cheer.

I guess, as long, as she drives the Bus.
We will have to put up with this "Pat".
She does a good job,
As far as I know,
And we do like her Dolls, Bears and Hats.

So let the Bus, continue to roll.
With Kind Jones a-steering the helm.
With time marching on,
And weather be damned,
Makes my corner a livable Hell.

1983

55

MY DAD * TERRY

The man I remember, was a gentle man,
Always helping, his neighbors out.
His house was full, of in-and-out friends.
It was fun, to have him about.

My father worked, in Cole' paper mill,
Chores at home, were always the rule,
Like raising goats, fixing up the house,
In the cellar, his live-bait pool.

My father so patient, with an impish smile,
Let us follow him, most every where,
And said, "You kids are sure a big help,"
But we must have "got in his hair."

Sometimes a penny, would come our way,
For helping, with all those chores,
And we couldn't wait, to spend it,
At the Main St. - Reds, candy store.

His days off were filled with pleasure,
Picking berries, cutting hay for goats,
Bank fishing, all the creeks and ponds,
Sometimes we'd rent a boat.

I would have liked, to have known my father,
As adult, friend, confidant,
Would liked, to have chatted, awhile with him,
Of his hopes, his dreams, his thoughts.

What was, he really like inside?
Would he, have told me his dreams?
Was he content, making five kids a life?
Would he, have answered me?

In some ways, I guess, I knew him,
Though I hardly knew him, at all.

1984

EXHAUSTED EXISTANCE

A mirror reflexes a stranger,
It is true and not true.
A lying shadow follow close,
Mocking in all I do.

Haunted eyes and soul, revealing pain
Of silent loneliness.
False desires form, burst, then vanish.
Dreams are nothingness.

The moon*lit false flesh body, walks
In dark timeless void,
Upon the unmarked, late-night sands,
Where waves use stones as toys.

Ghostly movements, yet looking back
There's foot-prints in the sand,
Revealing to me, I exist,
No matter who I am.

1985

TRAVELS

As my foot steps echo, in the London fog,
Along the banks, of the well-known Thames.
I love to stand, on the Tower Bridge,
And listen to old Big Ben.

I wander into, Trafalgar Square,
Near the National, Gallery of Art.
Knowing a feast, of Treasure's inside,
Will blind me, and fill my heart.

I enter, the Royal Albert Hall.
The largest, organ in the world,
Thrusts its music, upon my ears,
From the note-filled air a-swirl.

I browse, Convent Garden, Market place,
That sells, farm goods and flowers to all,
And spend a lazy, delightful day,
Sauntering 'round the various stalls.

In lively Paris, on the River Seine,
Ate in, Montmartre District café,
Where Lautrec and Chardin, painted canvas Art
Which hangs, in the Louvre today.

I saw Venus DeMilo, the goddess of love.
At the steel Eiffel Tower, I stood.
And walked along, the Champ de Mars,
Filled with beauty, and I felt good.

Then on, to drift down, Gondola Canals,
In Venice built on piles,
And stand on, the Prisoners Bridge of Sighs,
And be glad, I was not in their files.

Also in Venice, is Piazza Square,
Near the Bell Tower of St. Mark,
So I lounged around, the place all day,
Forgetting all time, until dark.

The city of Rome, was a must for me,
To view, Michelangelo's Art,
The Sistine Chapel, with ceiling so proud,
Where he poured, true love, from his heart.

I like to touch, gallant David, so tall,
And the Pieta, statue of two,
And St. Peter's where, I would sit all day,
In a silent, eye-wondrous, pew.

Across the water, of a sparkling sea,
I went to the Island of Crete,
Where Zeus was born, way back when,
And the Minotaur, roamed the streets.

The Palace of Knossos's ruins, are there,
Where Minoans lived, one day,
And some entertained, in the Palace Court,
As graceful, Bull Dancers, they say.

I finished my trip, in the Yucatan,
Among, the Mahogany trees,
And Maya Indian Temples, of stone,
Where the ruins of Uxmal and Izmel, be.

I've traveled this world, many a day,
And could do it, all over again.
I did it all, from an easy arm chair,
With my books, which I call my friends.

MANKIND

A Human was made as a miracle,
A mighty fine, rare piece of art.
He has a tough HEART and one HOLY SOUL,
And a BRAIN, which plays a rich part.

He can get through his life, nice and easy,
If he knows how to handle them.
The BRAIN learns first - some rapid - some slow,
What ever the person's trend.

He has the tough HEART, with its throbbing greed.
Spinning out his day-dreams and hope.
So fast a pace, he can hardly keep up,
And his nerves aren't able to cope.

He rushes head-long, into life you see.
No time to take stock as he goes.
It's got to be just, as he wants it, too!
All things must be his, like so.

Hey, there! Slow down, you've forgotten one thing,
Now the SOUL, must come into play.
I'm sure you'll remember, we have three things,
That make us a Human, God's way.

The SOUL is his price for living on earth.
Everyone, must pay his own way.
He makes his SOUL grow, or has a still-born.
It takes some control, everyday.

All it takes is wearing, some other's shoes,
And caring what happens to him.
Helping him out, of his ruts, he's got in,
Just having some moments to spend.

It's easy, if he would live by these words,
That I'm going to quote for you.
"Do unto others, as you would, have liked,
Those others to do unto you".

He's got to believe in the God above.
That's another rule for the SOUL.
It gives the life-everlasting to you.
A very life-worthy goal.

A Human can be a terrific thing,
With life-giving SOUL, BRAIN and HEART.
He can always conquer his wrongs and greed.
Each day on LIFE'S STAGE, play his part.

He can be an atheist, heartless and dumb.
He can be any ONE of these three.
Can also be good, fun-loving and bright,
And be what a HUMAN should be.

SEASONS IN LIFE

Seasons divide the years, into four parts.
They cast a spell, on everyone's heart.
The four have a beauty, all their very own,
Yet never the same, each one stands alone.

Spring starts life flowing, beginning of Birth,
World clad in Spring buds, and new green girth,
The winds blow hard, the warm rains will pour down,
A smile replaces, the cold winter frown.

Summer follows wished for, wet, lively Spring,
With picnics, vacations, meeting new friends,
A chance to relax, in the old lawn chair,
Getting a tan. "So let, the neighbors stare!"

Summer turns to Fall, with hardly a try,
The warm, "Gone so quick months", of fun flew by,
Summer colors change to a speckled hue,
Bright orange, yellow-brown, and fire-red, too.

The breeze fans your forehead and stirs the leaves,
The earth, waiting for sleep, "Don't say die, please",
Who can be sad with fall colors so gay,
Makes you feel vigorous, most of its days.

Old Man Winter gently trod along in,
With his cold and snow, his mighty North wind,
Covers this sleepy world, with sheets of snow,
Everything's white, with a beauty just so.

Icy rains, bend, the trees clear to the ground,
As the wind stirs, makes a snap crackling' sound,
Brings thrills to people, that play in the snow,
Others complain, they're so grumpy and low.

Not much activity, nature is still,
Just like she'd taken a good sleeping pill,
Waiting for Spring, when she starts to burst forth,
When the winds blow, from the South, not the North.

Each Spring and Summer, each Winter and Fall,
Showing life is like that, to each one and all,
Our Birth, Living time, our Sleep at the end,
To wake up again, with Souls, on the wing.

THE EMPTY CHAIR

The steam from the coffee,
Rises above the table,
Following the cigarette smoke,
And I look up.
Hoping to see someone,
Thru the contented,
Morning, sun-lit cloud,
Across the table,
But the chair is empty.

The easy chair is cocked,
At a lazy tilt.
With legs over the arm,
Hands holding a book.
My hand reaches for a smoke,
My head turns,
I start to speak across the room,
But the chair is empty.

I bounce thru the door,
Wanting to hurriedly tell,
Of the day's doings.
Little things I laughed at,
Who said what to whom.
I go dashing, chattering,
Over to the always sat at,
Dining room table.
But the chair is empty.

The much fought over,
Crossword puzzle stares at me.
My pencil flies,
Stops, hesitates.
"What is this word?"
I look up,
Not believing the no-answer quiet,
But the chair is empty.

I watch the bird-bath,
Filled with fine-feathered,
Noisy, sun-glistening splashes.
I laugh as the Blue Jay,
Commands that he be first.
And yell, "Here's your friend."
Stillness, no whispering slippers, I look,
But the chair is empty.

I drink my coffee slowly.
Gazing down the street,
At neighborly yards.
With undone puzzle squares
Lying, staring at the ceiling.
Knowing the tiny fun-filled,
Shared moments were lost,
Because the chair was empty.

1983

SECTION

II

A women's prison

I AM WHO I AM!

I stand, looking out of my long-narrow pane window, at the fenced in grounds of this prison.

Over the fence, sit houses with family doings and closely built apartments, with tenants sitting on the steps and visiting.

The one thing I long for is freedom and privacy. The simplest things, yet not important until they are gone forever.

I have my own room. Yet with thirty others on the same wing, it's not so quiet. The halls and walls, echo every small noise and dramatize the loud ones.

Even at night, on the half hour, the Officer flashes a light into the room, for bed check. Who wants someone looking, watching you sleep or snore? But it is for your protection. You might be sick or have a nightmare or try to hang your bloody self.

From early five-thirty morning, to "God, will it never come", ten-thirty Bed-bell, the building rings with steel banging doors, Buzzers, bells and loud argumentative voices.

Two wings of thirty rooms, each melt into the main Rec and Lobby looking like Grand Central Station, and twice as lonely.

Everyone steals your personals, cons you for your store-bought goodies, from the weekly commissary. Puts sneaky pressure to bear, till you join their group, for much needed protection. The "Families" dominated by a "Butch" sweep you into the group and you float along, serving your time as quietly, but not easily, as you can.

You let yourself become a walking, talking zombie, for all decisions are made, and all rules unbreakable. Every day, all the time you are serving, is exactly the same, boringly, the same.

You check off each long day, on the wall calendar, and know, each year has three hundred and sixty-five, "God, I can't do it", days. And know, that there are two more calendars to go.

I lie down on the bed, and wonder how I could have once, thought I was a "Boy, I can't get caught", clever street thief, and money-making drug runner. Yet knowing, that back on the apartment crowded street, the excitement will turn me into the one that's, "Ready for anything" crazy person.

I close my eyes to sleep hoping I don't have, a terrifying, screaming nightmare, and resign my self over to serving my short sentence, as easy as possible.

I smile, remembering, all the, before jail fun, knowing it's worth it, trading a few short years of jail, out of my Wild-night and day Go-on-forever, crazy street life.

FORBIDDEN JOYS

All forbidden things, of this world, are exciting, fun and curious, ever and always, making you feel, in that, "Who's goanna get caught" way.

Tiny tots playing Doctor, in the old Backyard clubhouse, or underneath the out-of-sight, sand bottomed shed, which leads to the Main Cellar.

The days of gleefully smoking, strong, stolen Camel cigarettes, while perched on the shiny ties, of the old D & H railroad.

We giggled and smoked in glee, for sometimes, stolen money bought, this hour of enjoyment, even though we coughed and spit.

The moments spent planning, which tree, should be the one, where we dug and buried, secretly, our coin jingling, coffee can.

And days of Hide and Seek, when the neighbor boy, always hid with you, and you wondered, why, you liked the quick, peck the cheek, kiss.

Older teen years, playing, laughing, upon the rocks at the Cave, then climbing the slick, wet walls, down to the rushing, spraying water. Going into the huge, limestone, ceiling-dropping caves, along the forbidden river bank, behind the old Paper Mill.

Being at the Village Beach, and swimming daringly across, the swift current river, alone, just to brag, to your dumb friends.

Or parking, necking in cars, in dark pine tree glades, feeling, "I don't care", "I can if I want", smug, very grown-up person.

Never dreaming, the reason, that all those forbidden joys, were only because, YOU, were loved, more than life.

THE FORGOTTEN ONES

The noise of the day had diminished, as evening settled down upon the New York City-owned building.

It was a small room, but big enough for the two that had occupied it for eternity. Anyway they looked that old.

The sterile room with the smell of disinfectant lingering in the air. Some floor tiles were missing, where the traffic was the heaviest by the door.

The two look-alike "cracked" ones never spoke to each other during the day. They just observed all the comings and goings.

Most of the people that entered the room, attended to their duties and left.

Some came in, took one look at the occupants and left saying, "Not this room!"

It was late at night, after the Security man had checked, before they decided to speak.

"Some day, huh?"

"There's a lot of off-the-wall gooks around here. How about the one that wandered in and fell asleep in the corner. Glad she was dragged out of here. Some of the women around here, look like they have been living on the street, or working on the street."

The first occupant sighed, thinking, "Lordy, it's her bitching day again. She talks about off-the-wall gooks, she's half off the wall herself." Remarking out loud, "This isn't ??? Ritz, my love. I'd leave if it wasn't for the bolts keeping us here. Nuts and bolts, that's us."

"You've heard that expression, "cracked in the head". I am!"

Speaking under her breath, the other said, "You can say that again, Honey. Cracks isn't your only problem. I have to listen to all the noises you make all day. Your insides gurgle and splash. Some days I have to put up with you letting water flow all over the floor."

Then in her normal voice, she said, "That's the reason for the bolts, to keep us altogether."

"Well, I can't stand the cold water bath in the morning. I'd rather not be cleaned, then be wiped with a cold rag."

Whispering, the other said, "Queenie wants her hot water. Call the court!" Raising her voice, "How about the one that came into the room and took out her needle. Sure glad she changed her mind and left."

"Wouldn't you think someone would check up on the floor mopper. His old string mop flings dirty water all over. I'm tired of getting splattered."

Under her breath, the other said, "Hear ye! Hear ye! The Queen doesn't want to be dirty." Then out loud, "The city doesn't care. We're old and forgotten."

"Once we were important! At least they give us our daily paper."

"Yea! And kept our room clean of germs. Disinfectant! Bah! I'm sick of the smell. Again in very low, tones, "I'm sick of her smell too!"

"I can't stand the noisy subway trains."

"Oh, you want to be over on Park Avenue? I'll tell the City Commissioner when he pays us a call."

Day-break was beginning to bring the sound of foot-steps, so the side-by-side occupants became quiet.

The door opened, exposing the Public City owned decrepit room and two look-alike, silent but broken-down cracked toilets. Where addicts and bag ladies took their leisure.

SCHOOL BUS DRIVERS

They roll over the roads with their steady hands and serious looks, not more than five or ten minutes, off the well planned schedule, dedicated to their job of carrying their precious cargo.

One thing I can't help noticing though, is they usually have their lips moving. I use to think, they were so happy on the job, they were singing to their darling charges.

But then I noticed more than once, that when their lips were moving extra fast, that's the time, the Bus would stop and the Driver would jump up and pass quickly down the aisle, waving her arms. I had a good idea, she wasn't entertaining them, by dancing.

Now, all of a sudden, my image of these beautiful people, who loves children changes to an ordinary human being, trying to make a buck, the hard way.

Male and female Bus Drivers have sudden quirks of doing odd things, reminding me of characters from, "One Flew Over the Cuckoo's Nest."

Listen:

One beautiful morning, the School Bus stops and Gram is kissing her kid Good-Bye. This leering male driver yells, "Where's mine?"

Playing along with him, Gram says, "Right here!"

Well, talk about Hungry Hank!

That Bus Driver unstrapped, raised from his seat and before his foot hit the last step, Gram had taken fright and flight.

One female driver, always has trouble negotiating her Right-hand turns. Everyone else whips around the corners with no problem, except this one, who makes a big deal out of it.

Putting on her blinkers for Right, she sits in the middle of Main St., waving every last car out of the side-street.

You'd think she was driving a double-hitch eighteen-wheeler.

Cornering, she runs the front tires, up to the left-hand curb and there she sits, stretched across the road, like a big yellow constipated canary.

Moving again she has all the action of a side-winder snake.

It's two blocks, before she gets the front of the bus, lined-up with the Rear-end.

Also we have a rodeo-circuit rider that decided to get acquainted with a Tractor-Trailer Driver and did it the hard way. She met him alright, after they entwined grills and bumpers, which wasn't very romantic, unless you enjoy seeing a School Bus and Truck making out.

Now we come to the confused Bus Driver.

One morning he just couldn't get his act together.

He stopped at every corner and asked, "Do you kids ride this Bus?"

Well, he traveled all across town, before he realized, that wasn't his route.

He acted like the "Little White Rabbit" in "Alice in Wonderland." Not quite sure what to do, knew it was something and late besides.

Most of the time, our Bus Drivers are steady-nerved solid Citizens and deserve three cheers.

It's just once in a while, they drive like a "Truck-Driving Irish Mick, full of Groats and Ale."

RIVER OF LIFE

Steady flows, the mighty river, between the shifting banks. Always forcing, pushing onward, making the waves rebel against themselves. Causing a swirling, twisting action that slops up over the bank, AND WETS ME.

As I lie lazily stretched against the river bank, I ponder about this river, which is like the stream-of-life, I am caught up in. As both hurry you along, it's either sink or swim and both eventually touch my life, AND WETS ME.

Timelessly sweeping along, moving everything in its path. Or leaving behind its debris, which escaped its strong current. Always in an everlasting rush, only to be disbursed among the Ocean salts, and lose its identity. A wave slaps a stone AND WETS ME.

I call the waters "Experience", as the sands wet by the water's edge, stands for me entering new life. The shifting banks lower me, slowly into the stream-of-life. As it laps my restless feet AND WETS ME.

Onward flows the river with these living sands. Leaving some behind from its long journey. The ones falling from the river's grasp lie still, forming the bed of the river, and their life is done. The stream-of-life rushes overhead, and rolls upon the sand at my feet AND WETS ME.

The waters swirl around and over, the treacherous I-don't-care sand-bars, leaping secretly out from the shore. As humans who cluster in groups, taking up negative space, not caring or seeing others pass. Then a spray, mists upon my face AND WETS ME.

It wends its way around thru, the Boulders and Dams, leaving them far behind. Reminding me of my coming trials, as I'm left to face them, everlastingly alone. Bogging myself down deep, in the current of strife. Angerly, I toss a stone, it splashes AND WETS ME.

Buoys peppered along the river, guide you to safety. As the churches on land wait, forever dependable. Glistening spires with their hidden bells. A bell rings, a wave breaks AND WETS ME.

I see the mighty river, greeting the ocean, at its open mouth, and dumping its living sands. And both waiting, at peace. Both knowing of death. I rise from the bank, wave, turn with tear-filled eyes, that fall AND WETS ME.

ALLEY TINSEL

As the slush from the side walk, seeped thru the soles of her make-shift shoes, Cora with her airplane design bag, was thinking of a wind sheltered alley.

Her walk was slow and labored, but had a determined bent. Turning the corner she spotted the shelter, "Good its still there."

Bending over she crawled inside, the gloom making her eyes blind for a moment. Leaning back against the wall, she hugged her bag and sighed. It was warmer here, she was glad she had remembered it.

These old wooden-cardboard cases were the home, intermittently of New York City Bag Ladies and wandering Winos.

Being tired Cathy slipped off into a cat-napping existence, until she started to cough. It was a lung racking, phlegm raising ordeal and when she was finished, she wiped her mouth on her grimy sleeve and leaned back exhausted.

"Are you all-right old lady," came from the deep corner of the box.

Startled she said, "I am sorry, I thought this place was empty. I couldn't see when I came in."

"That's all right. It's big enough for two. I've spent the night here and its almost where I spend most of my time. My name is Jack, what's yours?"

"Cathy, I usually stay across town, but the alleys have become too clean and its hard to find warmth in the winter. I use to come here a long time ago."

"If you see a policeman, don't worry because Mike watches over this place. He checks on us and brought us some warm blankets."

Throwing a dirty wine smelling blanket toward her he said, "Here cover up with this."

"You've got a real home here."

They both drifted off into their own dreams and were glad of each other's company.

Soon a pounding sounded on the crates over-head and a voice said, "Jack are you in there?"

"Yes Mike, and a friend Cathy is here too."

"Well, Merry Christmas you two," and the foot steps passed on.

"Merry Christmas? Jack it is Christmas Eve! The city will be busy today and tonight."

Thinking of past Christmases Jack said, "Cathy, do you remember any Christmases?"

"Yeah! Back when I was first married. A long time ago." and she drifted back to the days of youth and fun.

"Me too," and Jack thought of his merry, fun loving, Irish mother and the Christmas trees, she made for them.

Cathy started coughing again and couldn't catch her breath, so Jack moved closer, held up his wine bottle, "Here take a sip, it will cut the phlegm and help you stop coughing."

Looking at her face, he caught the sight of blood flecks on her chin, before she had wiped them off.

"You know Cathy we could go out and look at Christmas trees, and I could get another bottle of wine, a store friend gives me one once in a while and we could celebrate Christmas here, in our warm home."

Cathy's face lit up. Yes it would be fun to have company on the street. Then the young people wouldn't be mean to her, if she had a friend. They had set her Canal Street friend on fire one night, while she was sleeping.

"Yes, Jack, lets see Christmas together."

Crawling out of their box, they plodded toward the street, where life was busy.

In front of a bakery, was the most beautiful Christmas tree, they had ever seen. Millions of tinsel, blowing, glittering colored balls and small twinkling lights. Soldiers, Angels, Dolls and a little Manger with a baby in it.

As they stood there drinking in the beauty, each in their own thoughts, the bakery lady was watching.

Gathering up some fresh, warm goodies she opened the door and walked over to the "people of the street".

"You like my tree, I am glad. Trees are to be enjoyed by everyone."

Cathy turned, no one had ever just talked to her before, unless to tell her to move on or call her names.

"It's so shiny.", and she felt of the tinsel, so slippery.

"I love the little baby in his cradle," Jack said.

"If you want, you may take something off the tree to keep."

Smiling Cathy cupped her hands over some tinsel and gentle pulled it off.

"Would you like something else, to go with your tinsel?"

"Two things!" She spotted a red and white glimmering ball, "That ball would be nice."

The Lady removed the ball and placed it in Cathy's arithic, dirty hands. Turning to Jack she saw he was gentle touching the baby in the manger.

"If you like, you may have the little baby. That's the real reason for Christmas."

"I know, but I had forgot."

Jack held the tiny ornament so gentle, and turned to look at Cathy

Her eyes were bright, her toothless mouth was grinning and she said, "Merry Christmas, Jack. Merry Christmas Bakery Lady and thank you."

"Merry Christmas to you both and take these goodies to eat this Christmas Eve."

Turning away Cathy and Jack started down the street to get the bottle of wine from his friend.

Arriving back at the boxes that were home they crawled in, smoothed out the old raggy blankets and then leaned against the wall. Feeling chilled, they pulled one up over their legs and lap.

Jack opened the wine and sat the bag of bakery goodies between them.

They were getting warm and the street light let in enough light so they could see. Glancing at Cathy, Jack begin to laugh, for Cathy had draped the tinsel on her head, and was holding the ball in her lips.

"I thought I would look as pretty as the tree was."

"Cathy you look real nice."

They were warm, the wine, the goodies gave them a satisfied feeling and not being alone was peaceful.

"Cathy can I hold your hand?"

Sitting together holding hands, both drowning in memories of long ago, they napped and day-dreamed.

"My back hurts Cathy, lets lay down and cover up."

Getting comfortable took sometime, as their bones ached.

Jack felt a pain stab him in the arm, but he thought it was arthritis, until another shot across his chest.

"Damn gas, I'm not use to rich food."

He soon had to think about Cathy for she was coughing again. Harder this time and was exhausted afterward.

"Were you ever married Cathy?"

"Yes, once and he was so handsome."

"Me too, a long time ago."

Both reliving their dreams, they moved closer to each other.

Jack didn't care if Cathy was old, wrinkled or dirty. Her body felt good to him. Soon Jack was dreaming of his wife so beautiful, until she died in childbirth. In Cathy's mind it was a young, strong husband of long ago.

Jack gave a sharp cry and Cathy came out of her dreams and looked at him.

"It's only gas, Cathy, but it sure hurts."

"Lets just lie together holding hands, Jack. I feel so tired now, and its hard for me to breathe."

Lying down again they soon fell asleep ending a Christmas Eve that was filled with sparkle, good food, nice people and love.

Christmas Day Mike pounded the crates in the Alley and hollered, "Jack you there?"

No answer.

Bending over and looking in, there was two empty wine bottles, two people lying close, amid bakery paper, and a familiar airplane designed bag.

Cathy's mouth was bloody, but she held her tinsel and ball in one hand, the other was holding Jack's and Jack was clutching the baby in the manger.

Mike drew the blanket up over their faces and with blurry eyes, whispered, "Merry Christmas, Cathy and Jack, at least you weren't alone."

SINGING EYES?

Small boys were throwing snowballs upon the porch of an old unpainted house and chanting, "Old Mrs. Cook. She looks like a Witch."

With the opening of the house door, the boys moved slowly back away from the house.

Leaning on two canes, dressed in a black dress, that hung loose upon her bent, arthritic, seventy year old body, she admonished the boys.

"Go on home and stop dumping snow all over my porch. Your mothers will hear about this."

Jeff looked at his friend, "Why do you call her a Witch?"

"Cause her hands are like claws and all crooked, like Witches in books."

Jeff stood staring at the woman and didn't notice his friends had left him.

Looking at the lone boy, Mrs. Cook hollered, "You get out of here, too. You hanging around to make more trouble?"

Turning and walking down the street, Jeff thought, "His Grandpa's hands were all crooked, too. He always said how they hurt all the time. Mrs. Cook's hands looked like Grandpa's and he wasn't a Witch."

Grandpa was shoveling when Jeff got home, and seeing the kid hollered, "Grab a shovel, and help clean the walks."

"Grandpa is Mrs. Cook a Witch?"

"She wasn't when I went to school with her. Why?"

"The kids throw snow at her house and call her names."

"I'm sorry, Jeff. It's not right! Let's make her eyes "sing"."

Hearing a scraping noise out on the sidewalk, Sarah Cook stepped to the window.

"Well, I'll be!"

Pulling the curtain aside, she remarked, "Who's that old man? And that's the kid, that kept staring at me, after his friends left. Well, if they think, they're getting' paid, those two have another think coming."

Finishing the walk, Jeff went up and knocked on the door.

Opening the door Sarah heard, "I'll be keeping your walks clean this winter Mrs. Cook."

"I can't pay you."

"That's O.K. Grampa says if you do something nice for someone, you make them have "singing eyes"."

"Singing eyes?"

"Yep," and Jeff ran off to catch up with his Grandpa.

As Sarah closed the door, she muttered, "What the duce is singing eyes."

With a slow caned-help walk, she went to her comfortable chair, took her tray of wood and tools upon her lap and started carving.

Sarah knew her carvings were not the master pieces she had once produced, but it made long evenings pass quickly.

Pausing, she rubbed her aching hands, musing "I wonder if that boy would like one of my birds, for helping me?"

One day hearing the school children pass by, Sarah went to the window to see if Jeff was among them.

Spotting him, she opened the door and when Jeff looked up, Sarah motioned for him to come to her.

"Want something, Mrs. Cook?"

"Come in, I have something to show you."

Following him into the living room, Sarah said, "What's your name, you seem to know mine?"

"Jeffery, Grandpa calls me Jeff."

"Well, if you don't mind, I'll call you Jeff, too."

As Sarah was getting seated, Jeff walked over to a shelf, that held a few of her carved birds. He gazed at each one.

"Did you buy these?"

"No, I carved and painted them. That's been my hobby most of my life."

"They're so pretty. Can I watch you carve."

"O.K. you bring my tray of wood and knives to me and also bring that bar of Ivory soap, sitting on the table. I'll carve you a soap bird."

Jeff was all smiles as he handed her the tray. Then sat down in front of her to watch.

"By the way Jeff, what did you mean, when you mentioned "singing eyes", the last time we talked?"

"Grandpa says, people's eyes "sing", when they're happy."

"You mean they make music?"

"Nope. They don't make any noise. They kind of shine. Grandpa says, we have a machine in our head that makes our face talk.

If we're happy or sad, this machine knows and makes our face happy or sad.

Grandpa says, most people say eyes shine, but they don't. He says faces shine, but eyes "sing"."

"What does the machine do when people are sad?" Sarah asked, dropping soap chips, as she was carving out the beak of the bird.

"Grandpa says, then the machine sends a cloud over the face and it looks dreary like on a rainy day and sometimes the eyes make rain."

Sarah repeats, "Grandpa says, Grandpa says. Sounds like you and Grandpa do alot of talking."

"Yea, he's my friend. He tells me about a lot of things."

"So Grandpa says, if you make someone happy, their eyes "sing"!" Holding up the finished soap bird, Sarah said, "Well, what do you think of my bird?"

Taking it in his hands, Jeff caressed it carefully.

"It's lovely, Mrs. Cook. It's real Jim-dandy."

"O.K., you take it home with you. Now, that you've watched me, maybe you can carve one yourself."

After Jeff had gone Sarah realized how alone her life had been lately.

A couple of days later, entering Christmas week, Jeff pounded on Sarah's back door. Out on the porch-railing, was a home-made bird feeder.

"What's going on here Jeff?"

"Well, you like birds, so me and Grandpa made a feeder, so you can get to know all the birds. It's our Christmas gift to you. We put it on the porch, "Cause you can get to it easier."

"It's the nicest bird feeder ever. Come in for a moment."

Now was the time to give Jeff the bird, she had carved from wood for him.

"I have a Christmas gift for you also, Jeff," handing him a box.

Jeff was stunned, there sat a bird on a limb, with his head cocked to one side, and holding a sunflower see in its beak.

Letting his fingers feel the wood, he looked up smiling, whispering, "It's the bestest."

Carefully setting it down, he drew a wrinkled package from his coat pocket.

"This is yours too, I bought it for you."

There amid the wrinkled paper, lay a small hand mirror. On the back was a picture of a bird flying.

"Oh Jeff. This is so pretty, I'll use it every day. Well, my friend, you have given me two wonderful gifts. Thank you very much."

Jeff looked into her face saying, "Now you can see your eyes "sing"."

Then brushing her cheeks with his lips, he was gone.

Sarah held the mirror up to her face, and remarked, "Grandpa's right. Eyes do "sing"!"

Then as a tear rolled down her cheek, she sighed, "Grandpa's singing eyes, rain too!"

She laid her head back and chuckled, "I guess its called 'singing in the rain.'"

A MAGICAL SECRET

Once upon a time, when the world was just beginning to grow trees and grass, for the first time, there lived a little girl in a big dark cave.

This cave was her home, because it protected her, from all the big wild animals.

Her name was "Light-in-the-sky", because she loved to watch the sun and the clouds as they traveled across the sky.

Sometimes when there was no animals around, Light-in-the-sky would leave her dark cave, lie down in the grass and watch the clouds.

One day a soft voice, sounding like music asked, "What are you doing?"

Turning her head, Light-in-the-sky saw a beautiful lady, wearing a white dress and a big pair of silvery wings. In her hand she was holding a stick with a star on the end. The star flashed and sparkled a light as blue as the sky.

Light-in-the-sky said, "Hello, I'm watching the sky. I love to see the clouds dancing around the sun. It makes me happy. What are you doing? What is that blue star?"

The white lady smiled and said, "I'm helping Mother Nature. I am an Earth Angel and my star is a magic wand. I am suppose to plant berry bushes, so the birds can have something to eat, nut trees for the squirrels and special plants for your people to eat."

Light-in-the-sky asked hopefully, "Can you make something as beautiful as the sun and clouds? Could you have it grow, right here down in the grass, where I can touch it?"

"Your talking about flowers. I'm not suppose to make flowers. Another Earth Angel is making flowers."

The little girl looked sad, "I sure wish I had a flower as yellow as the sun and as white as the clouds."

The Angel felt sorry for the little girl.

She said, "If I make you a flower, will you promise not to tell. Also I shall have to ask the flower not to tell. You both must keep our secret."

Jumping up and down, Light-in-the-sky laughed and said, "I promise, I promise."

"Now," said the Angel, "Stand still."

Over the little girl, the Angel waved her magic wand with the flashing blue star, than touched each one of Light-in-the-sky's feet.

"Today we will make a very special flower. Every where in the grass you put down your feet, a beautiful flower will grow. I will follow you and touch each flower, so it will know, it can never give away our secret."

Light-in-the-sky danced around and around all over the grass, and the Angel flew behind her.

Everywhere the little girl put her feet, there popped up a flower, as yellow as the sun and with petals as white as the clouds.

Soon Light-in-the-sky stopped dancing and picked a flower. It was so beautiful. She turned to thank the Angel, but the angel had gone.

For many, many summers Light-in-the-sky would walk among her pretty flowers. She would touch them and say, "We can't tell, we got a secret."

Even today little children look at a flower as yellow as the sun, with white petals like the clouds and say, "Daisy's don't tell!"

A DAY IN "TIME"

The Correction Officer reached for the ringing phone. "Officer Ball, here."

"Lt. Dunn speaking. Report to the Administration Building to process two inmates. The Sheriff's just brought them in".

"Yes, Lt."

At the state's Women's Prison, Officer Ball left the cement-block, high-on-a-hill building and walked to the Administration Building. She entered the processing room where the two inmates were, with their bags of personals.

She glanced at one and was looking into the eyes of her sister's child. Without any emotion of surprise, she turned to the other, and started the strip search.

Checking clothes, listing everything on slips, and re-dressing her in Quarantine clothes. She called the Escort officer who was to take her to Quarantine Floor.

Looking toward the other inmate she said, "So you made it here at last, Susan. Let me advise you on a few things. For one thing, you'll get along much better, if you don't let anyone know we are related. Also let me warn you, you thought you were tough on the street, but in here you'll come up against tough you never heard about.

You might never be assigned to my floor, after you come out of Quarantine, but if you are, don't expect any extra favors from me. I have rules and you have rules."

"Don't worry cop, I can take care of myself", Susan said with a sneer.

"What's your time?"

"Zip three."

"so you'll be paroled in eighteen months. I am glad it's a short time."

"Who cares, I'm sick of all you cops."

"Just remember, us cops, so you call us, didn't put you here?"

A Month later, Susan was assigned to the very floor her Aunt controlled.

Officer Ball worried over Susan, because her floor was dominated by two "Butches" and their families. There never was any trouble or fighting as neither Butch wanted any of their women to go to the Segregation Floor.

Officer Ball and Butch Mary had been on the floor for five years. So one day she went down to Mary's room to talk.

"Straight talk, Mary. We've been together a long time and I'd like to ask a favor of you."

"Sure thing, Officer."

"I know you've noticed the new kid, Susan, that just came to the floor? She's my niece. She thinks she is tough and I don't want her in trouble, so her record is clean, when she goes up before the Parole Board. I want you to take her into your family for protection, and I don't want you to take her to bed. What work and goodies you get out of her is your business."

"Ah! Come on, you know I bed all my women, when you cops aren't watching."

"Not her!"

"Damn, you come down hard."

"I know if you give me your word, you'll stand by it. You've broke up a lot of fights on this floor for me, and we've both been fair with each other. Do I get your word?"

"Yea, yea," standing and pounding the dresser top. "Only because your one fair cop and you try to solve our problems, instead of putting us off. Yea, I'll make a bargain with you. I'll talk to Susan today."

"Thanks Mary."

Before Officer Ball had got back to her office, where her co-worker was, and argument had started in the Recreation Room. Susan was screaming nose to nose with an inmate.

Before the Officer could reach the couple, Mary had the two of them separated and was leading Susan down the corridor.

Flinging Susan onto the bed, Mary bellowed, angrily, "What the fuck, do you think your doing? Do you know who the hell you were fighting with? You snotty-nose kid, you could have got in real trouble, and made the rest of your time here real bad. That cat was the head of a family and we don't mess with each other.

Right now, she thinks you belong to my family and that's the way it's going to be. You belong to me and you're going to pay off with cigs, food and keep my room clean."

"I don't need your fucking protection"

"The hell you don't, you dumb-ass. We know your Aunt is the Officer here. Us inmates get our news our way. Those inmates will set you up to fight. You'll have so much Seg. time you won't get out for three years. Just play it cool, Baby, and old Mary will protect you."

"I hear we bed-down with you for pay, too?"

"That's right Baby, when I say meet me, you better come. I pick "chickees" that I trust, that way I don't worry about those cops catching us. Man, it's going to feel right nice to have a new cat again."

Susan jumped up off the bed, "You fucker you."

As she passed Mary, Mary grabbed her by the chin, "That's right women, your all mine. By the way, I smoke Winston's."

Following Joyce out of the corridor, Mary caught Officer Ball's eye and winked.

The Officer mouthed the words, "Thank you."

"This is a work of fiction. Names, characters, places and incidents either are the product of the author's imagination or are used fictitiously, and any resemblance to any actual persons, living or dead, events, or locales is entirely coincidental."

A SMOLDERING FUSE

Hearing the sound of footsteps outside the door, Sue changed from a relaxed body to one on alert, tensing each muscle.

Bob was back.

He made her world hateful.

She knew that soon there would be verbal and physical abuse.

Sue and the kid could sometimes avert some instant confrontation, by keeping on the farthest side of the small cabin.

Lumbering through the door, Bob had that old familiar smell about him.

Weaving toward a chair, he noticed his slippers were over across the room.

He exploded, "Can't you ever leave anything alone? You don't touch anything of mine. Damn you!"

He walked across the room, gave Sue a kick and pushed the kid against the wall, stooped and picked up his slippers, which were where he had thrown them last night.

That was mild abuse.

The worse part was mistreating the little kid. Sue tried to protect him as much as possible and only got more abuse.

Her hate grew and she knew someday she would kill him. Her eyes burned with hate. Her time would come.

She had something to fight with but didn't want him to be turned ahead of time.

Early one morning Bob started punching the kid around, swearing and throwing things at Sue.

He slammed her into a corner and she knew this day was the end of his life.

When Bob turned his back to go for the kid, Sue came flying out of the corner, and threw all her body weight onto his back.

Bob went down.

She hung on, driving her sharp weapon into his neck. As they rolled around the floor Sue's desperation made her cling to his body.

She stopped mangling his neck and turned her weapon onto his face. She couldn't stop.

Both of them was covered with blood. Bob's face was ripped, pieces of flesh hanging, his throat torn, before she realized that he wasn't moving anymore.

Sue stood silently looking at him and went over to the kid cringing in the corner.

She gave the kid a kiss and they started toward the door.

Outside the kid put his arms around her neck and after a moment they walked down the road.

A young boy and his dog, Sue.

EGO - MANIA

Flying back from the sunny South, with the wind behind them, they traveled with an easy saving of energy, Sailing over a house, with a garden of Morning Glory's and Milkweeds, they dipped their bodies and perched on an old rail fence.

"Well, Hummer, I'm glad you know this area, food for you and food for me," softly spoke the Monarch Butterfly.

"Let's eat and then I have more to show you, my pretty one," and the Humming Bird went toward the Morning Glory's.

"Hey Flutter, come over here and sit, the old lady is watching us. Let's show her how beautiful we are."

Giving the old lady a few minutes to look, they took off.

"Let me show you the town now," Hummer said, flying close.

"You know I hate traffic, the cars whirl the air and I get caught in the drafts."

"You don't have to get that close. They've got window boxes high on the second floors and we can sit there."

In the middle of town, they perched on a street sign and looking down Flutter saw the dead body of an other Monarch Butterfly.

"Oh! Hummer. Look! She's dead. Her wings are bent and all her beautiful dusty colors are faded. Do you think that will happen to me someday? I don't want ever to lose my beauty. I want people to stare and caress me with their eyes. I know I'm beautiful and I want everyone to see me that way always."

"Flutter, I caress you with my eyes, cause I think your beautiful."

"I don't want to fade ever. I want to last for eternity."

"Now don't get morbid on me Flutter. No! It's not going to happen to you. Stick with me and I'll take you to safe places."

Sitting on a flower box, watching the town's busy part of the day, Flutter couldn't get the scene of the dead Monarch out of her mind.

She knew some year she would die, but now it was very vivid to her.

She glanced at her wings and knew she was just about the beautiful thing in town.

She lashed out at Hummer, "I don't want to get my wings broken, and I don't want to lie in the street all faded."

"For gosh sakes! You still harping on that subject. Let's go up to the next flower box."

As Flutter settled on a flower, she glanced in the window. Sitting at a table, facing the window was a small boy working on a case of his butterfly collections.

Flutter watched him carefully handling them, looking at them with eyes that admired their beauty.

She thought, "He cares about them and even though they are dead, they still have all their colors. That's better than being in the gutter all broken."

"Look Hummer! Aren't they something else?"

"Jeepers Flutter, they're dead and they have a pin through their body."

"I don't care. That way I could always be lovely. Hummer the windows up a little, I'm going in."

"No! He'll catch you and you'll be doomed."

Her proud egotistical heart saw it differently, so she fluttered across the sill.

As her body lifted off into the room, a net held her, then she felt a sharp pain in her back, and darkness over powered her.

Hummer watched, with tears in his eyes, as the boy added Flutter to his collection.

"My proud suicidal one, I shall miss you fluttering beside me. It wasn't enough that I thought you were beautiful. You needed more."

Flying out over the town, the words, "Damn you", drifted behind him into the air.

UP IN THE AIR

"How can some people, think riding on a parachute is fun?

Boy! I'm scared stiff!

I wished I'd never thought about going up in the air and floating down.

If I had known, what a feeling it would have given me, I surely would never have been mixed up with this thing.

Better hang on to this string, with all my might!

My, but the wind sure blows hard up here.

The land looks so far away. Ooh! I can't look down.

Must cling tight and ride this contraption down.

Keep my head at all times.

I hope I reach the ground before long.

Gee! they say you really hit the ground hard, don't float down too slow.

I suppose if the wind catches this thing, it will blow it across the ground. Bumpety-Bump!

Wonder if I'll get hurt?

Well, I sure know what it feels like.

Don't think I'll try, to ride around in the air again, for a while.

Gosh! I'm getting dizzy, flipping back and forth, in this wind.

Makes me wish I had some honey to wet my mouth and throat, kind of' dry.

Am I glad, down to the top of the trees now.

Won't be long, before that jar to the ground."

So then, the Butterfly, very gracefully, flew off and promised himself, never to ride on a kite string again.

AIR-BORN FOR AN ETERNITY

"You'll never get me, on a faster and safer way to travel, plane".

MY WORDS, which today I shall be forced to eat. To fly, is one thought that makes my false-teeth quake, even on the dresser.

I have no pioneer desire, to travel faster than sound, or to be any higher than the third rung, of a step ladder.

The fast, dive-in-and-out of traffic cab, delivers me at the airport, way before I've had time, to muster up my courage.

I stand in a ticket line, stiff with fear and move only when the person behind, pushes my not eager body forward. I groan, as I realize, I never did buy my dope-me-to-sleep pills.

A smiling hostess, drags me to my seat beside a window. Lucky me! Now, I can watch myself, fall down thru the clouds, after the engine fails.

After we're air-born awhile, I glance at my seat buddy, for some reassuring words, and find him sound asleep. I hate his irritating peace, and dream of tasty revenge for him.

Glancing out the window, my staring, bugged-out eye balls are level with the wing and I know, its molded of tin-foil.

"My God, it wiggled". A loud vibrating noise pounds in my ears, like the wing is rocking. Thru the noise, I notice my chin hurts,. My spastic mouth is open, and what I hear is my false-teeth chattering, against the window rim.

The ou-to-get-me hostess, who's smile turns into a leer, suddenly becomes the Hansel and Gretel Witch. She hands me something to drink, but looking at her, I know somewhere her cauldron boils and bubbles.

After the plane lands, from its faster and safer way of travel, I find my air-born rubbery legs, are carrying, an adrenalin-less hundred year old carcass, with a bruised chin, and a cracked false-plate.

SWATS AND RUNS

A group of my athletic friends, had a very active commitment, to spend our day off, breathing that fresh country air, that has a myth about it being cleaner than city air.

I'm not sure about clean, but I would have just as soon had it vacuumed of those whining, flying straight-up-the-nose whirl-i-gigs.

Being in a field, under the hot sun, getting dirty and drinking tepid water, is not my idea of having fun.

Thinking of a lawn chair and beer, I put on my best ecstatic image, as I look toward the field.

Passing thru the fence, I know this is not going to be my "live-it-up-in-the-open" day.

We put all of our gear, we brought, into a pile within easy reach.

Soon it's time to begin and our fun work starts, with lots of hollering and hooting back and forth.

"Damn that fly, I should have had it, that time. How come every time I get my hands up to catch it, it moves two more feet away?"

"Golly! There goes a ripping run".

"Well, I struck again at that sucker and missed. I knew it would happen".

I'm beginning to feel like the Martyr Joan of Arc and I'll be burned as crisp, from this sun.

Walking, feet dragging, back to the water, even tepid water is an oasis, I find my friends have emptied the jug.

That made my day!

I'm so dry I feel like 4he Arizona Santa Ana Wind has been blowing on me for days.

"Lucky me!"

Why couldn't I have had friends, who thought that too much activity was debilitating and all the energy they were ready to put out, was just enough to keep their eye-lids open.

As I sit hot and tired, disgusted with all those beastly runs, also mad because everyone else is hooting away, having a good time, I dream of a "Tom Collins" and don't even have energy enough to dream up the ice cubes.

Right then and there, I promised myself, NEVER EVER to go into a fly-infested field, to pick Blackberries again, especially wearing Panty-Hose.

SCORN AND REVENGE

All day I've found myself, being drawn down into a pit of gloom.

Black suffocating clouds, so hate-filled they swirl around my body, entering my nostrils and lungs, infecting my Brain cells and turning my Heart, cruel black.

I feel the full, awesome power of Hate, which makes me into a blood thirsty, unfeeling, cold, Devil-woman.

As I crawl, sobbing between the covers, and lie here in the dark, cruel scenes flash before my red-rimmed eyes.

I day-dream of being able to stand, and spread out my arms, above the world, and point a power-charged, your-next-to-suffer finger of Revenge, on my adversaries. This fills my heart with the utmost glee.

To pick and choose from any living, smug human alive, and cut loose my power. Not to kill, that would be too quick. Enough to maim and torture, causing all kinds of suffering. Just enough, so they almost reach their breaking point, then I would stop.

Making them continually aware of all the pain. So now, for once, they are busy with their own dilemmas, and their busy tongues are crying their own pain.

I shall then walk away and stage my last cruel act of mercy unto myself.

Take one soul, I care about, and force them to quickly and cleanly, shoot a fast, non-feeling bullet, into my Brain to explode. Forever ending all my hurt feelings from some smug, narrow-minded slobs. As my executioner pulls the trigger, award that soul the peaceful sleep of Death.

Hoping, healing sleep will drug, my fury-spent body, I turn over, my tear-soaked pillow, and thank the "Almighty" for making me a weak, powerless Human.

LOVE MAGIC

The no-see phantom-like vision, glides constantly before my eyes.

Never blocking the view, but always taunting my active, romantic, wishing heart, for things which can never be.

It hangs in my mind-room, like a "Mona Lisa" print, though only a melt-in-a-crowd face.

The passing person in-the-flesh, holds my eyes like magic. The not-mine-to-have face smiles, and impish eyes beckon, causing my liquid heart to spill. The aching happiness, furrows a frown upon my brow.

My non-hearing ears are silent, my feet take root in the earth. Yet my hands ache to lie, against the everlasting dreamed of face.

My incoherent tongue voices, a greeting of sorts. A smile cracks two frozen cheeks, giving my face a foolish, turn-of-the-century robot look. My "love" passes along, leaving me a happy mass of aching confusion.

Brighter now burns my vision. Night and day following me, always there, flashing before my praying, wish-you-were-mine eyes.

Every night holding sleep and dreams at bay, in my darkened room. My heart screaming, pounds out words of reason, "Let it go. Let it melt into the swirling air, to become a torn, mis-shapen streak."

I lie my tired-drained body, against the pillows knowing, the everlasting vision will always be.

BEMIS LAKE

Rippling waves very gently lap at the shore, of the small lake, nestled snugly at the mountain's feet, resembling a huge mirror.

The sunshine helping, reflects the purple mountains and white clouds, upon the blue, Sail-boats-blowing-like-leaves, lake.

Near the waters edge, a secluded, hid by a hedge small dream cottage, with its big picturesque window, looks out at the friendly-night, city lights, which wink back at you.

Spending happy, relaxing, dreaming days, you promise to return, with your true love.

But never, quite make it.

NO "GRAVE" VISITS

Don't mourn for me, over a field of cold, shining, summer sun-glint, or winter snow-capped granite, for I am not there.

I roam free over the land, and wait patiently for your joining. The rest of your years, spend forever, carefree, lived to the fullest moments.

Put no flowers, on my decaying grave. It won't brighten, the cold dank hole, but remember, the field of rare trillium, like stars, we viewed on a hillside.

Remember, the snow-bent, ice-coated trees, touching the new fallen, trackless snow, tunnel arched, over a dirt, least traveled road, one cold morning, new dawned day.

And the sun hot, wave crashing beaches, where waves captured a pair of well-liked, summer sandals, and the careless tide, carried them off to nowhere.

And we stared together, in wonder, at the eye blinding beauty, of a sun ripened, waving oat field, wearing a crown, of no-cloud in the sky blue.

And on a mountain top, a clothes grabbing wind, forced us to descend early, but not before we rock-sat, exultant, with our head in a low cloud.

Don't be, I-never-could-stand-you sad. Enjoy your fun, crazy earthly joys.

If need to, once in a while mourn, happily mourn, by smilingly remembering.

IT CAN'T BE!

My sad pencil, writes across this sheet of paper, carrying a "This is it" message.

This note will sever two friends, who enjoyed a long, couldn't be closer friendship.

You think, we can still be, "Just good old" friends, but it's not for me.

"I love you", too much. Your love, was not ever, supposed to be mine.

Your hand-touching nearness, brings pain and watery-blinking eyes.

You'll remember me, as a "use to have friend", and I'll remember you, "My Love", as a rare and precious gem.

THANKS FOREVER

As I walk along the street, kicking Fall leaves, I don't, can't believe, our long friendship, is finished, by death.

So busy and short a time, yet long enough, to live an exciting life.

Where everyday was a wonderland of discovery.

I loved you, for you loved living.

Filling your soul, with the beauty of the world and having a child-like, excitement about everything, you saw, felt or tasted.

You filled my life to over-flowing, and made me grow, into a very aware, proud-of-myself person.

I shall humbly cherish, what you gave me. It will always be mine, forever.

OVER COFFEE

Her words floated, circle 'round the room, some forced-fed with anger. Tear-filled, with a hopelessness. The sound crackled, bounced back and forth until falling on my ears.

The furnace heart within was feeding, suppling, the ever flowing energy of fire. Which was bursting the seams, of her proud, loyal, complicated ego.

Moments, of not understanding, were confusing the feelings of her youthful, married, child-born and dream filled body, were so mixed. As having been fed into a butter churn of long ago.

My ears strained to hear the ever, heavy-laden words, which were not being spoken. And my mouth emitted sounds, to help, console and comfort her bleeding self.

I cradled her in a surrounding of soft, gentleness, caring, understanding clouds. And let her spent, relaxed, aching body, slowly mend its self with an inner peace.

Her blue pained-gazed eyes changed, turning her face into a picture, of her smiling, ready-to-trust self. For my absorbing heart had listened patiently.

The caring words and the smile energy, with a gentle helping hand, were mine, over the table to send. For I listened and helped a friend.

YOU TOOK THE TIME!

When you heard the "good news", you made time, especially for me, out of your family-busy, fast-paced, hectic work-a-day world. Just so you could show me you cared, and say you were glad for me.

I looked up hearing my name spoken. I saw you standing there, with your smiling face, and shining eyes.

You were as excited over the "good news" as I. The caring moment filled me with rapture, for having a friend, who cares.

I love you for sharing my dream and really caring about how it progresses. My dream is only a hobby, and I shall never be money rich. But my life is far richer, then ever before, for having known you, my Friend.

WHEEL-CHAIR PRISONER

I sit bound, to this nuts and bolts metal chair. Even if they didn't strap me in, I no way in hell, could move a muscle.

My body is frozen, unmovable, with a pair of eyes, to show emotions. A clear-thinking brain, which can't communicate, thru a hung-open, drooling, unsightly mouth.

Visitors look at me, full of pity, sadness, horror, then drop their eyes. Hoping, they won't have to look, at my slackened face.

"Look at me! I need, want, someone to show me, you care".

I look around, and only see, white-sterile cold walls.

"I wish I could just once, stick out my defiant tongue".

"I don't want to die".

"I'm too young, too scared".

"Nobody cares out there."

Five years is a long time to be held prisoner. I sit, a victim of M.S. Strapped to a wheelchair, and wait for unstoppable death, in this Nursing Home, and pray it's soon.

NARROW MINDS

This small Northern Town, reeks of bigots, practicing their loose mouth bigotry. Slandering whole races, of different humans.

Never seeing each one, as an individual, and not ever wanting, too. Hard, cruel, sneering words, smoking on a viperous breath of "I am better than you" air. Hot from an egotistical, mouth. "Spic" - "Pollock" - "Kike" - "Nigger", and many more, cause my ears to burn and my temper to boil.

Who put these snobs, so high the thin air makes them foolish-minded? Most of these pure-white bigots, were American born. Therefore, never had to overcome language, class, color or strange cities.

So I say to them, "And what have you done today?" "What big mark, have you scratched on the world?"

Immigrants and born slaves, became giants, that walked this land. They earned Doctorate's and Awards, with their years of hard, maddening toil, over coming great odds. In research labs, and making inventions, which saved lives, and broadened our minds.

And so you W.A.S.P. Bigots I say, "Kneel humbly", and tell us what to inscribe, tomorrow, on your cold, forgotten Tombstone.

SILENT TRUTH

The old man sat in his rocking chair on the porch. The Funeral had been this morning and he wanted to be left alone to think and rest.

So many years, so many days of hard work with her. Now she was gone.

He thought about the house and all the changes he had done on it.

She always was busy and he had done everything she wanted.

She wanted and he gave to her. Always improving, always needing, that was her way.

Busy, busy, morning 'til night.

She was determined to have something and went after it like a "top sergeant".

So many years, his whole life time and now it was over.

The old man leaned back in his chair, the house was quiet now.

He had all the time in the world.

Lifting his beer bottle, to his lips, he drained it and with angry vengeance threw it into the flower garden.

Snarling, "I hated you, May!"

TOO MUCH TOGETHERNESS

Funny thing how you want something so bad, you know you'll die without it.

That's how he felt, once.

In the beginning it had been a happy time. The hours of being together, of savoring each delicious moment. As time passed he begin to lose interest. There was too much togetherness.

His wish had come true and now he would like to be out of this situation.

So tired of being clung to.

The pressing against his lips and his face, was something that irritated him now. He thought to himself, "I don't want this anymore."

So tired of having himself bound to a mess.

"I've got to get rid of this frustrating nightmare!"

"Enough is enough!"

"I'll end it now!"

"Be rid of it forever!"

He turned and spit into the road, his sticky wad of Bubble Gum.

INEVITABLE

For months now, the constant clinging, hanging on, had changed.

At first it was a game, a challenge, to see who would out last the others. The sap of life flowed, keeping vitality and combating old age.

Now, everyday it seemed like the pace had picked up, and weakness galloped in, making a listlessness and a tiredness.

Trembling, shaking movements in the dried up body, with a pale jaundice color, shouted the end was near.

The swaying and weaving had started again. Spinning crazily in the darkness, with a force so strong, there was no denying, that time had run out.

With one last shudder, the line to life was broken, and there was a detached feeling of floating.

Lifeless, drifting downward, the last pale yellow leaf settled, onto the moonlight, new, fallen snow.

WANTING AND GETTING

I take the old, wrinkled, torn, faded letter from my pocket, to re-read. For the millionth time.

Yes, it's there, written in ink. A solemn promise, to breakfast together, at some futuristic time.

I had visions, of clean, white, newly pressed table cloths. Linen napkins. Silverware and napkin rings, and a vase of small blue violets.

Shimmering, sunny-side up eggs, with a green sprig of parsley. Making the bacon and eggs, into a good-morning Bouquet.

Waterford juice glasses, holding sunny orange juice. Along side of a slightly toasty, warm Crescent Roll.

As time wore on, I thought it would never be. But one warm summer-like, late winter day, the phone rang, giving me the delightful date and time. I was thrilled, excited.

A day later, we appeared before, the brightly-lit, garish building of the Golden Arch.

AUTUMN

Roads winding thru colored wonderland, slowly creeping up the Mountain heights, then hurrying steeply downward, never leaving Autumn glory, very far behind.

Colored masses swirled together. Yet colored individually, as though the colored dew, off the rainbow, sprinkled shades of every hue, upon the world, with the help of the gentle wind.

Each mountain top resembles a huge bouquet, that old mother earth hands her children. Just to see if their eyes will turn misty, make their throats breathless, and fill their hearts with happiness.

Sun-light giving every leaf a glory of its own. Letting them have their last big fling, before the fall rains dampen their spirits.

FASCINATION

As the sky was slowly drawing, its Evening Curtains, a dark storm was brewing, like a demon mad at the world.

The powerful and dangerous wind, had the black-gray clouds racing madly, toward nowhere. Snatching and grasping, clearing a match-stick path, across the earth.

Thru the racing clouds, jagged lightening tore, and sharp clap thunder emerged like a Lion's roar.

Then the hard steel rains, beat heavily to the ground, and drum pounded, against the window, where I stood watching, in an awe, spell-bound trance.

Written with

"Tongue-in-check"

and

"Fire-in-the-Belly"

I am so glad -

to read my Daily Paper which contains the page, "Letters to the Editor".

I am so glad -

to see we have many intelligent and feeling people around our area, who set themselves up as Judges.

I am so glad -

to see our "animal lovers", so torn up and protective of disgraces and hurts forced upon the animal kingdom.

I am so glad -

to see that so many people know the Bible so well, they can quote "God's Word", to every situation.

I am so glad -

to know we have so many "self-taught" medical men, that knows what makes people tick.

I am so glad -

to see they sign their letters with their real names.

Because -

it makes me realize that there are still "Witch Burners" out there, ready to throw another log on the fire.

Because -

it makes me cringe, to know that people still love animals, much more then humans, as it takes too much time to love people and you have to give of your heart and they know their heart isn't big enough.

Because -

it makes me not forget that there is people ready to crucify and gossip with their flappy tongues.

Because -

I know then, that people are still fomenting "Holy Wars", instead of spreading love and joy with an understanding, caring heart.

Because -

Then I can stay away from them with their narrow-distorted-minds and their "Better-than-me" egotistical attitudes.

Because -

I know then, how many people were never taught "Love thy neighbor as thy-self" also "Judge not, or you shall be Judged also".

#5 RIVER ST. - GRAY

The quilt patterned, tic-tac-toe streets, of the above-the-river hillside Village, cuddles the houses close together, leaving a squeezed up, grass patch lawn.

An old, well-lived-in, sand cellar house, nestles on a back, once sand street. Lording it over unpretentious, short-histories homes, knowing it's had a long-memories life.

The changing paint, weather-beaten gray house, once towered over, a one-man one horse farm, kid cracking Hazelnut bushes, kid stealing fruit trees, canning vegetable gardens, and farm animal coops.

Fields became sand dug-out, board-top club houses, hoarding secret stories, treasures and doings. A fun-filled, "Look what I got", dump, rounded off the sand bank corner lot.

It stood the test of people bulging walls. Of changing open rocking chair porches, to screened-glassed private cubicles. Common sense tin smothers the cedar shake roof.

The tight planned four room downstairs, held a family of five, three-born-here, kids. The inside-outside stairs, leading to the ever rented, two family shared bath apartment, still goes on.

As the family grew, they encroached upon, the kicked out renters, for made over bedrooms. The play-sleep downstairs bedroom, now houses a full tabled, Sunday chicken dining room.

Over the kids leaving, returning years, the open door, safe, harbor house, has welcomed, kept rent free, many from each, come back generations.

Each needy generation, snuggles within, and with memories pouring from its sides, it captures them, protectively, until they restlessly move on.

The towering, proudly, will-lived in house, turns its smiling paned windows, onto the crowded street, and knows there is more to come.

1984 CHRISTMAS LETTER TO MY KIDS

Merry Christmas Kid,

This money is to bring you some kind of happiness. Spend it in a way, which will bring you joy. Either on yourself, your home or another person.

Not knowing all your wishes, I know you will pick out a present more to your liking.

Although I hate to give money, as I like to buy my gift, you will get money this Christmas Day.

The best present you can give me this Holiday Season is a better rapport among all of you children.

All "one" has to remember is that each of us has flaws, because we are human. If we were perfect, we would be saints, but alas this can never be, and I like you very much just as you are. If you didn't have faults, I couldn't holler at you and I like voicing my opinion once in a while.

Everyone likes to hear the words, "I love you". It takes only one breath to say, one opening and closing of the mouth, one lifting and lowering of the tongue, and one second to make the recipient and you feel rather good about yourselves.

Your gift to me will be from a mind that thinks, a heart that loves and a soul that thrives.

God Bless You All,
Love, Mother

GRAM'S (FOR TEENAGERS)

Gram's are relaxed, and they take up their place, between the now and then years, which we all call, the Generation Gap.

Going to visit and talk, is like stepping into a space, of stand-still time, relaxing and warm.

She knows, understands, your young mixed-up problems, are serious, and have a painful soreness.

She knows your loves, are important and listens, thinking of her first true love. She never says, "You're young, you'll heal". Just lets you talk, and some how her ideas, become yours.

We lie in bed talking, and she touches my hand, or puts her arm across my pillow. Soon we're laughing over sick jokes I remember from school, and jokes on my friends.

When the house is full, on the Holidays, and the beds are all over the floor. We tell stories or give Gram our science lecture, or show wrestling holds we knew.

In the morning is the best, for we all climb onto her bed. We all try to get under the covers, by pulling someone out of bed.

Everyone helps with breakfast. She always says smartly, "The one who breaks the egg yolk, gets to eat the flat eggs". But somehow or other, the flat ones, always, end up on her plate.

She's young enough to enjoy our music, try our new dance, yet old enough to know, one minute, we are adults, and the next foolish kids.

Knowing we're not perfect, she gently encourages, the things we do well, and pushes us onward to adult-hood.

DANNY WITH GRAM

Dear Mommy and Daddy,

My day at Gramma's house.

Boy! This house is neat. Do you know I can walk all the way around the house! It was neat.

I checked her flowers out, but she was watching me. Oh! well, maybe I can get them some other time.

Then she opened a draw and pulled out many little things to play with.

Now its time to go to the corner to help school Bus Kids. She got on all of her clothes - orange vest and all. Boy she looked like a penguin.

What a time she had getting me in the car seat. For one thing she can't buckle the straps without swearing, and she hurt my crotch, so if I never give you any grandchildren - its her fault.

That's not all the things she put me thru. Parking the car! Yep, right in the sun, and leaves me. Well, if she would rather talk to those kids instead of me - who cares! So I went to sleep.

Want to know what else she did. Coming upon the porch - she banged me in the face with the door. You call that a baby-sitter? I didn't cry because I'm a big boy - right guys?

We pulled our clothes off and settled down to a picnic. I had cheerio-oats and banana also toast with peanut butter. Gram had shredded wheat and toast. Some friend called her on the phone, but Gram took her cereal with her. Boy, I could have had fun with that. As it was I stole her toast and carried it around the house with me, till she got off the phone and ate it. Mushy and all.

At last she gave me my juice - I thought I was in the Gobi Desert, I was so dry.

I sat under the T.V. set for awhile, like having my own little house.

Walk - I walked so much I was getting tired. Did Gram noticed? Nope! I laid my head down on the couch, fell asleep and toppled over on the floor. I laid there, until Gram put me up on the couch. I'm tired at 10:45 - yawn! (Bet Grams glad!

12:00 p.m. I'm awake, but I guess I'll lay here awhile. I feel lazy. There's Gram sitting in the chair reading. She's so engrossed, I bet its pornography.

Well, it looks like she's going to change me again. She'll find a surprise - I pooped. Yep, I did, serves her right, feeding me all that bread and peanut butter.

Lordy I'm not hungry and she's coming with more food. Dinner time? Who cares! I didn't eat any.

We sat and watched T.V. rocking. I don't feel very energetic. Gram called in on her job. She lied and said she had a sick baby. Bet you it was cause she didn't want to fight the car seat again. Saves my crotch again.

Whoopie, I got her cigs. Short lived whoopie, she got them back. Damn.

A nice afternoon, I walked around, sure getting my exercises.

2:00 P.M., Dad should be here soon.

Bye-Bye,
Danny

P.S. - Ate dinner at 2:15, I'm a good boy, huh:
P.P.S. - I pooped again - lucky me.

WRITTEN BY 1 YEAR OLD JUSTIN

Dear Mommy and Daddy,

What an evening! So Gram came again to do her duty baby-sitting.

The first part of the afternoon was all just as it is suppose to be. A loving Gram and three nice little kids.

We finished our burgers and then Gram escorted us to the swings. About the burgers, I finished Peter's. He left it, so finders keepers.

The swinging got a little boring, so Gram, Sharon and Peter played ball.

They thought they were going to get me to play kickball. Imagine kicking a ball and chasing it, what a dumb game. Two kicks and I left! I'm not that stupid!

While Gram and the kids were playing "Simon says", I figured it was good time to make a "bee-line" for the wood pile.

Treasures! Did I find some treasures! Two beautiful cigarette butts. You know how I admire those things. I stood there gloating and giggling. Was just going to put one in my mouth, when this big hand appeared in front of my face.

I thought God had reached down from the skies. Well, I did! I've heard big people say, "God will get you for that."

When that hand grabbed the butts I turned and saw two legs. God doesn't wear jeans, so much for trying to have a good time.

Then Sharon and Peter got into the hose fun. So Gram let them fill my cart with water, and from then on was the best time all evening. Nice gooey-splashy mud.

Good times always stop especially with Grams around. We could really take care of our selves you know.

Gram turned her back and was picking up the yard, so I climbed upon the back porch, and I spotted the flower urns. The same feeling came over me, just like when I found the "butts". You can't help your self. Honest!

I looked up to see where God was, no God, and gently lifted each plant. I was so good at pulling them up. They came so easy. All of them.

Sharon saved me that time. Wow! She told Gram she learned in Girl Scouts how to plant, so she pushed them all back. I could have done that with a little more time.

I recommend all Mommies and Daddies should send their girls to Girl Scouts. Especially with bored little boys in the family.

That was Gram's cue, or excuse to think about taking me into the house for a bath.

I don't know how it happened but next thing Gram knew, Peter and Sharon had their bikes and were out in the road.

Boy! Was Gram mad. She shoved me into the kitchen and started hollering.

I knew the fun had begun. I raced around the house trying to see out the windows. Gram was mad, I knew something exciting was going to happen. It. did!

She collared those kids, lifted them off those bikes and they walked home.

Sure they cried, who wouldn't. Why can't Gram understand how much fun it is to ride in the road.

With all the bawling and talking going on I heard them say, "I hate you and your not coming down here again".

Do you think that hurt Gram's feelings? No, sire!

She said, "I don't expect you to like me, I'm punishing you and want to bet I'll be back".

She sure has a way of topping you, she always wins.

One thing more I recommend, put in windows down low, so 1 year olds can see out. I missed most of the whole thing.

Well, between the bawling and arguing she got us two boys clean, only I pulled one last dirty trick. Yep, you got it - I had pooped my pants. Gram even spoiled that fun, she never even wrinkled up her nose.

I recommend for the last time, that when people get married, they pick out Grams that are nervous, so little kids can "get their goat". Then we could have more fun.

Your sweet loving Son,
Justin

P.S. - I hate being a tattle-tale, but maybe it will get rid of Gram.

POT * HOLE CROSSROADS

Vic, singing off key, cruised his eighteen- wheeler, "Honey Bear" along the desert high-way, when spotted a figure walking along the shoulder.

As the miles closed in, Vic wondered why a young girl would be way out here walking.

Hearing the truck behind her, she turned and held up her thumb.

Slowing down, Vic was kind of glad, for having company was an added bonus on this long, flat country, barren road.

He threw open the cab door, waiting for her to catch up and climb in.

"You going into Vegas, Mister", was spoken standing on the gravel.

She was pretty, petite, a little dirty and was carrying a kids athletic bag.

"Yes ma'am, and your welcome to ride along, just as long as you can sing and talk. I need Company".

"Thanks Mister. Thanks alot. I can sing, but I might fall asleep. I got dumped last night, and I've been walking ever since".

Climbing in she slide down in the seat, relaxed and closed her eyes.

"How'd you get dumped?"

"A real down-right sex maniac wanted pay for his ride and I wasn't up to that much excitement. So he got mad and pushed me out".

"You running from something?"

"Yeah! A husband that uses me for a punching bag, has girl friends and thinks I should be there to give him his dessert in bed, when he comes in early in the morning. Well, I kind 'a got tired of being used, tired of no love or kindness and figured if I was going to be a prostitute, I might as well make money at it".

"So here you are!"

"Yep, Las Vegas has loose money and I am going to get me some. Then I'm going to live like other people, own an apartment, get nice clothes and I'm going back to school".

"How much schooling you had?"

"High school".

"What you want to be?"

"Art teacher, I paint good!"

She settled back and started humming to the radio. Vic liked her looks and dreamy, hurt but fighting spirit. Soon she started singing and he knew, this was going to be a nice trip.

"Your voice is very good, done much singing".?

"My Pa and I always had jam sessions. He played guitar with both of us singing. He died a year ago".

When Vic parked the trailer just outside of Las Vegas, she was sleeping. His "Honey Bear" was a sleeper, so reaching up, he got a blanket, laid her over in the seat, and covered her. She looked so child-like and pretty.

Climbing up into his bed, Vic realized he had enjoyed this trip very much, and would be sorry to see her go.

The minute Vic woke up, he leaned out of his cab-bed and looked down into the seat, and looked into the grayest, twinkling eyes he had ever seen.

"You were hoping I would be gone, but I'm not. I would have started coffee, if I knew how in a cab", she said teasingly.

"Our kitchen isn't far away, I'm parked in back of a diner. Jane is a good cook. We can clean up and eat, before going into town. She has a shower and rents towels to us boys".

"Are you insinuating I'm dirty?"

"No, no, my lady, just knowing you'll feel better, after a nice shower with dial soap".

She threw the blanket at him and bounced out of the cab.

"By the way lady, what's your name, mines Vic"?

"Kate".

"O.K. Kate, lets bathe and eat".

Jane looked up and smiled when she saw Vic, he was her favorite, a damn nice kid. then she frowned, when she realized a girl was with him. She was pretty, but a little bit hard looking, "A hitch-hiker, I bet".

Vic was sitting at the counter, talking with Jane, when Kate came out of the shower.

Vic turned to motion her over and stared a moment too long. Her natural curly hair really liked what he saw, smiling he got off his stool and held out his hand to her.

"Jane this is Kate, she's going to Vegas, to seek her fortune".

"Well Kate, all I can say is Good-luck. Your not the first to stop here on the way in, and I usually get a chance to say good-by to them on their way out".

"I'm not coming out Jane,

I'm going to school, after I get a job and study to be an art teacher. I know it won't be easy, but I'm responsible for my life now, and its going to work".

"Give us a good bacon and egg breakfast, Jane. It might have to last Kate all day", Vic said, smiling at Kate.

Jane turned to the grill, and thought, she talked different then the others, and there's a quality about her I like.

Looking around the room, Vic spotted two girl friends, excused himself and left for their table.

For the first time Kate felt alone, she kept glancing at the table, watching them talk, and spotted the girls looking at her, while Vic talked.

"Is one of them Vic's girl, Jane?"

"Nope, Vic doesn't have any girl. Believe it or not he's waiting for someone special. He helps all his friends out, men and women alike, but never loses his heart. There are plenty that have tried, but he's a waiting man. He's all heart."

She thought about how he never laughed at her or any of her ideas yesterday and how gently he covered her up in the cab, when she was only half asleep. His smiling face when he was teasing her.

Coming back to the counter, he said, "Those girls are prostitutes in Vegas, Kate. Now, if you want to, they will let you stay with them and see if they can get you a job, where they work. They'll teach you the ropes and help you. I asked them to look after you and they will, because they are my friends. They told me to send you over to their table, when you have finished eating."

"I don't need them."

"Yes you do, that place will eat you alive, unless you know what your doing. I don't want to read your obit in the paper. O.K? Kate, I like you and want to help you. If you ever need me, meet me here. I have this run once every week. Please take care of yourself. If your ever hungry, Jane will feed you and I'll pick up your tab. No strings attached! You understand?"

128

"Your a swell guy Vic, I like you."

"Thanks Kate, leave a note with Jane and let me know how your doing."

Filling up on eggs, bacon, home fries and toast and laughing together, was the nicest time Kate had ever spent in the company of strangers. Strangers yet it seemed like everyone dared about each other.

Bidding good-by to Vic, Kate turned and went in the direction of Vic's friends, the girls that would help her.

"Hello Kate, sit down and join us. As soon as we finish our coffee and cigarette, we'll be off," said Kay.

"Thanks, what's your name?"

"Kay and this here is Jerri, we are to help you get started and we will. Vic always gets what he wants with us two. He has befriended us many times, with us he is the cream of the crop".

"Hello Jerri. I'm glad to have your company, Vic sure is a nice guy".

"Well, some girl will be damn lucky, I wish it could be me", responded Jerri.

The girls finished up, paid their bill and said good-by to Jane.

Climbing into a little red convertible, they headed for Vegas.

Kate wondered what was ahead of her, but knew she had to make a go of it, if she ever got what she wanted. She did want it!

Parking behind an old, wooden, white, stately Hotel, Kate said

"Well Kim, here is your home and job center, if you want our kind of work. This long wing here, is where 6 of us girls live. We each have our own room and bath. The rest of the house is where we entertain. Some times we have to go out on a case, but usually we work here.

Come and meet our Boss, but if I know Vic, he has already called and told her were coming. She cares for him as much as Jane does".

They entered the lobby and a beautiful, graceful, woman was leaning against the piano smiling.

"I hope you girls enjoyed your days off, and Kate I am glad to meet you. Vic says your out to make your fortune and if money will help, you'll make it here. You'll get so much a week ad a percentage of the house. If you want this kind of work, I'll be glad to hire you". You will call me Miss Bea".

"Thanks, Miss Bea, I'd like to try it", and Kate shook hands with her.

The girls got Kate settled in, went out and bought her clothes on Miss

Bea's charge cards, then filled her in on the different jobs, they would handle.

"You know Kate, you get creeps sometimes, but they are customers and we are here to serve. What ever kind of loving they want, they get. Miss Bea, nevers allows us to be beaten. That man never comes back in here, nor does she take any outside cases from him. An outside case is going to the man's hotel room".

Kay stopped speaking and the girls left Kate to her self for the rest of the afternoon.

Evening found them in the big living room, where drinks were served and the girls were entertaining the customers. Kate noticed, that as soon as a man took a fancy to a girl, they disappeared up the stairs. Wondering who would pick her, she felt a hand on her arm.

"If you can stop staring into space, for awhile, I should like you to join me in a cocktail".

Turning her head she was looking at a well tanned, full bearded, smiling face of a man about 60 years old.

"Thank you, yes I would love to join you for a drink. I've had such a busy day, I guess I was wandering a little".

"You're new here, aren't you?"

"My first day".

"You're pretty and have a nice shape, you should last a long time. Miss Bea makes her girls comfortable and takes good care of them".

They sat at a table drinking and talking, with the customer first patting her arm, then rubbing his leg against hers, then letting his hand rub her thigh.

She knew soon he would escort her upstairs and she started to prepare herself to what was coming, "This is my first, and by god I will make it. Think of it as just a job, Kate, don't get personal with it, and think about the money".

The customer gently took her arm and nodded toward the stairs.

As the door closed, he softly said, "Take off your clothes, and lie on top of the bed. I can't have sex like normal men, I had an accident in W.W. II, but I still like to look at a women's body and feel of it. If you get excited and groan, that makes it nicer, for me, because then I feel like I can still turn on a women."

Kate was thinking, as she undressed, "My God, this is sure an easy trick. I've faked it so much at home, I ought to be able to blow his mind."

As she laid on the bed stark naked, he laid beside her and gently let his hand drift slowly over her body.

Kate steeled her mind and body, knowing she had to make good this time and maybe the rest of the evening would be easier, because of it.

As he rubbed, and pawed her body, she went into her act, of motions, and paused breathing, then enacted her vocal groans.

She glanced at him and he had his eyes shut and seemed to be in a trance.

Soon he just laid back and gave a big sigh, but Kate never moved, not knowing what else was coming.

She had no more worry, he got up, dressed threw some money on the dresser and turned to take one last look at her.

"Thanks lady, I'll see you again."

Lying in bed after her first busy evening, Kate wondered if she could really do this as a living. It wasn't her bag, yet she wanted that money. Did it get easier as time went on? Why did so many men, even married ones, need to come to Miss Bea's? Do you get use to being used, even though you were getting paid? Why does it feel as if you don't belong here, like something isn't right?

At the end of the month, the only thing that kept Kate working was always looking at her bank-book. She had a nice pile saved up and it was now time to sign up for college. Her morning courses, wouldn't interfere with her night work and she had an old second-hand car to use. In one month she was on the road to realizing her dream.

One day Miss Bea called her into the office.

"Kate, you've done a nice job for me, and I've had good reports on you. Thanks for cooperating with me. How's school coming?"

"It's great, my marks are up and I love every minute of it. I have to thank you for giving me a chance, so I could have my dream."

"Don't thank me. I needed you and if Vic hadn't asked me, we would never have known each other. I have a special job for you tonight, out on a case. I don't know the man personally, but a client recommended him. It's extra money for you, want to take it?"

When Miss Bea had mentioned Vic's name, Kate was thinking, I haven't left him a note, and I sure would like to see him again.

Half in a fog, she said, "Yes, I'll take the case and thanks".

Going back to her room, she wrote a note to Vic, knowing one of the girls would be going out to Jane's tomorrow, and would leave it.

Dressed up for her evening, she hailed a cab, gave the address to the cabby and relaxed, thinking of Vic.

Getting out in front of the Hotel, she entered and found the apartment. Thinking, "God what's behind this door", she knocked.

The door swung open and there stood a professor type man. He was clad in an oriental robe, smoking a cigarette held in a lavish holder.

Smiling he spoke, "Good-evening Kate. My name is Dan. Your smaller than I pictured, but your beauty makes up the difference".

"Why am I small to you, you must prefer tall woman?"

"No, not tall, just big bones, there is more strength in their arms".

Not replying, Kate thought, "Shat in hell does he want strength for. Am I to have, to wrestle him to the rug, force sex on to him".

Dan walked over to the bar and took out two glasses, "What do you drink, Kate".

"Vodka and orange please", and she glanced around the room. It was very beautiful, done in white and blue, almost a little too feminine.

Taking Kate by the hand he led her to a back bed-room.

"Let me show you and explain how I want my evening to be spent".

Carefully laid out on his bed, was a whole array of black and silver objects.

He carefully picked up a black leather jacket and mini-skirt with silver buttons and an over-sized silver buckle.

"You will wear this tonight, because I think black is a dominant color".

Glancing at the bed, Kate held her breath. There were black-high heel boots, a small whip, and a thick silver studded glove.

"So you are into pain, is that the evening activity," whispered Kate, as her breath slowly exhaled.

"To you Kate, it sounds sick and disgusting, and I guess it is. No one knows this about me, but it is necessary if I am to exist as a functional human in the outside world. I can only have an orgasm, when the pain is intense enough. I need that moment as much as any human needs an orgasm in love making. You are going to be my lover. Have you done this before?"

"No."

"Even if I bleed, cry or twist with pain, you are not to stop. You will know when I am done. That last moment is worth all the pain, believe me."

Kate started donning the clothes and Dan disrobed showing a beautifully shaped body.

Lying on the thick rug on his stomach, he instructed Kate to start lashing at his shoulders and working down to his buttocks. After lashing his torso, she was to put a boot on his back and beat him with the studded glove on his buttocks.

Kate inhaled, shut her eyes and swung the lash.

"Harder, harder make it hurt," he gasped.

Trying not to hear or see Kate began a strong, systematic series of blows up and down his back. Driving her boot down hard, she forced the studs on the glove into his rear.

With his cries, pleads, groans assailing her ears, confused concentration, and building up a tremendous swear, Kate lost track of time.

A scream, brought her out of her fog, and looking at Dan's rear, shocked her completely.

As Kate saw the open cuts, the blood running in rivulets, her stomach started up into her throat. Turning and running toward the door, she never stopped until she stood on the curb in front of the hotel. Hanging on to a sign post, she emptied her body of all disgust and then cried for Dan.

As she entered the wing, going to her room, Kay was walking toward her.

"O, my God! You got one of those cases?"

"What makes you say that?"

"You're still wearing the black suit."

"I left in a hurry, I couldn't finish it Kay. I was sick. I've got to get out of this business, I feel all the pain of my customers, and every day I let myself get a little closer to feeling a disgust bout myself. This trade is not for me anymore. I'm going to talk to Miss Bea in the morning."

"I'm sorry Kate, we'll miss your friendship around here. You've become a part of our family, don't forget us, O.K.?"

First thing in the morning Kate knocked on Miss Bea's door.

"Well, Good-morning Kate!"

"Miss Bea, I ran out on the customer last night. It was a black-boot-whip affair, and when I saw the blood running down the buttocks, I got so sick I ran outside and vomited on the curb. I cried for that man. I have got to leave here. My emotions are ruling my head. I want you to know, I was truly grateful for the job, the chance to make money and all the kindness you have shown me."

"Kate it's not a surprise to me. I knew you were different. You see, you came here with a dream, that kept you going, against your real feelings. If I had known the nature of the job, last night, I wouldn't have sent you. Where do you go now?"

"Back out to Jane's Diner, see if she needs help. I'm still going to college. If no job there, I'll look around town. Thanks again Miss Bea, I won't forget your kindness and I'll be seeing you and the girls now and then."

Saying good-by to the girls was painful, as they had been her family and again she was on her own.

As Kim parked in front of Jane's Diner, the smell of food was tantalizing and Kate realized she was very hungry.

She took a seat at the counter, noticing the place was full and only Jane was on duty.

Jane was putting a plate down on the counter, when she spotted Kate.

"Well, I said I would say "good-by" to you on the way out. Or is this a day off and you want my conversation. How would you like to help me out for an hour, I could use it?"

"Sure why not, anything for an old friend".

Kate grab a pad and soon was busy serving the tables. People kidded her and also found fault, but Kate liked the give and take of the strangers, and MaryJane was a good teacher.

As soon as it quieted down, Kate sat at the counter again and ordered her food.

"Well, Kate that was a big help, and for the first time being a waitress you sure can hustle. I'd offer you the job, but your use to big money now, and You'd die of boredom out here."

"You know Jane, I was going to ask you for a job, I've left Miss Bea. I can't take that pressure anymore."

"You are different, Kate. I knew that when you first came here with Vic. O.K! your on! Start anytime you like. What about school?"

"I'll change my subjects to nights next semester, there's only a week left in this one. I have an old jalopy to go back and forth in, but I'll have to find a room somewhere."

"Kate just before you enter Las Vegas is a few houses that rent rooms. Try them tomorrow. For tonight you can sleep on my couch."

"This must be my lucky day, I've got a new job, maybe a place to live and my dream still goes on. Jane you and Miss Bea are good-hearted people."

"Want to hear something that will surprise you. Miss Bea and I are sisters. No one knows only you and Vic. Vic is Miss Bea's son. His sister died at the hands of a mad man, hitch-hiking home from town one evening. That's why Vic helps out so many young ladies. He's paying a tribute to his sister."

Jane got busy and Kate slowly and thoughtfully ate her late lunch.

Work at the diner was hard, but fun. Her room at the Boarding House was cheerful and school became a goal to fight for.

The next three years were full of fun, new found friends, dates with school professors, and dates with Vic, until his trucking run was changed about a year ago.

Kate knew Vic liked her, but he always kept himself very much removed from any commitments. It was always "see you around", "I'll call when I hit town."

Her fourth year Kate was substitute teaching. Her third grade class kept her on her toes and sometimes she laughed with tears in her eyes, at some of their expressions.

One day in the teachers lounge, she glanced out the window and stood watching a trailer truck unload. She recognized Vic and ran out to see him.

As she neared the truck, she was a little nervous, for she knew he was closer to her than a friend. She had thought about him too often.

"Hello Vic, its been over a year."

"Kate", and he picked her up hugged her, but as he set her feet on the ground, he forgot to release her.

"Kate, I've missed you, you look so good to me. What are you doing at this school?"

"Sub-teaching, to finish my degree."

"So you made it. You've got guts and your smart."

"I know."

Staring into her face he slowly let his arms drop and held each one of her hands.

"Teacher can we have supper together? That is if you don't have another date."

"Yes Vic, we can, its been a year and we have a lot to talk about."

"I'll pick you up about six. You at the same boarding house?", and he slowly let go of her hands. "Your pretty, Kate!"

"Well, Mr. Vic, those are the nicest words you've ever spoke to me. Absents makes the heart grow fonder? Yes, I'm at the same place. See you around, trucker!" and with a smile she turned toward the school building.

Sitting in the fancy restaurant, they were sipping their wine when Vic spoke.

"Kate, you've made your dream come true, with hard work and I'm glad. I knew you world, way back when I dropped you at Jane's Diner. I knew your teaching degree was very important to you, and over the years seeing you on dates, I've let myself think about you a lot. I never said anything then, because I wanted you, to do what you wanted to, with your life. I always hoped, you would find time for me once-in-a-while. Now, your about finished with college and no man has captured you yet, so I would like to ask you if you would consider me for your exclusive date from now on. I cared about you three years ago, and I have been falling in love with you, ever since."

"Vic, I've had a special place for you ever since the beginning, too. Why didn't you tell me? You didn't want to tell me till I got my head straightened out, did you? Vic I love you, for your gentleness and understanding. You know something, Mr. Trucker I'd be proud and honored to have you for all my future dates."

He stood up, crossed to her chair, put his hand under her chin and gently kissed her.

"Lets dance."

Holding each other, as they danced, they both knew they had left, their pot-hole cross-roads behind, and would travel the main artery forever, with love fogging up the windows of the Eighteen-wheeler, "Honey-Bear." Especially on teachers two month summer vacation.

FEELING FREE

The lovers had been planning this for a long time, only the two of them, and today was the day.

Dave leaned over, gave Chris a kiss and then they settled their bodies as close to each other as possible.

"I know it took you a long time to decide to do this Chris, but I'm glad you over came your fears."

"It's very exciting being wild and crazy, Dave."

She moved against his body and wrapped both arms around him.

Laying her head down on his shoulder, Chris whispered, "I love you."

"Just being here, has proved that."

Over the day, their excitement melted into an easy feeling of knowing each other. Taking them from cloud nine to a lazy tiredness.

Dave watched her walk across the room, and begin laughing.

Chris turned, "I can remember when you just looked at me with stars in your eyes, now your laughing at my bow legs."

"No, not your figure, it will always put stars in my eyes, just that your starting to walk like a sailor. You've got sea legs."

"Dave, what do you expect? Most of the day all we've done is had our bodies in a straddle position. I'm not use to having my body beat to death. You know something!" and then softly, today was the most beautiful time, I've ever spent. You've gone out of your way to show me new things, and I've loved the quiet lazy times, when we took time to rest and talked."

"Tomorrow is our last day, Chris."

They curled up together and fell into a peaceful sleep.

The next day was as exciting and as lovely.

As the sun begin climbing high in the sky, Chris was beginning to feel the heat. Her body was sweating and her hair was so wet it clung to the nape of her neck.

"Please Dave, lets stop and have a cool drink. I could stand some cooling down. Besides my muscles are lame and sore. You didn't tell me I had to be an Olympic athlete."

When she came back with her drink, Dave spoke, "We only have about three hours left, and our togetherness will be over. Two whole days of getting to explore, talk and just be together. You might not be an athlete, but your a good sport and I love you very much."

"Dave, I wanted to do this as much as you. We made a good team. I love you and I'm going to be sorry when it's all over."

At the end of the day, Chris was tired and sore, and was beginning to think she had been crazy to spend that time with Dave.

She didn't think she would ever ride a motorcycle again, touring Arizona .

A SHORT SPIN

Eric put down the phone and walked to the window. Staring into the street, he sighed, knowing the days ahead would tax every emotional nerve in his body.

Annie had asked, if she could stay at his apartment, until she got her feet under her. Annie and Joe had been his friends and now they had spilt.

He had loved her once, before her marriage, but she had wanted excitement. She always challenged every minute of every day, for she loved living.

Again he would have to hide his feelings from her and again watch her leave when the time came.

Could he play the friend part? Could he control his physical body? He must or open old wounds.

The door bell rang.

Taking a deep breath, he opened the door, "Annie welcome to your new pad."

Dropping her two suit cases she threw her arms around him.

"Thank you Eric. I won't bother you, or disrupt your life. I'll be as quiet as a mouse."

"You a mouse, how can a whirl-i-gig all of a sudden become a mouse."

"Well, I'll try."

Eric laughed, as he picked up her suit cases and went into the guest room.

"The room is yours as long as you wish."

He left her to unpack and went back to his papers on his desk. Being a professor was exciting to him, but it entailed a lot of boring papers to mark.

Coming from the kitchen she sat a glass of wine by his papers, "To our friendship, which is very dear to me."

"Thank you, Annie, and to our partnership."

"I'm trying for a job in New York City with a jewelry company, photographing models wearing their gems. It'll be a big step for me, so wish me luck."

"Why New York City?"

"Start a new place with a new beginning. Life begins at forty remember?"

"You'll make it Annie. Your good at your work and you know fashions. A toast to your future. May it be as you wish."

A couple of weeks had passed and Eric had enjoyed having Annie around. Her erratic bouncing in and out, preparing crazy suppers consisting of sprouts, squids, foreign foods and garlic -plenty of garlic.

One night Eric was awaken by Annie crawling into his bed.

"Please Eric, let me sleep with you tonight. I can't get to sleep, I'm scared I won't get that job, I keep thinking of my life with Joe and I feel like a gypsy. I just want to be near someone. Let me lay on your arm."

Eric extended his arm and she curled up by his side.

"You're pushing your self too hard and too fast. Tonight is your night of doubts. On doubter's night we get scared, we get lonesome and all we do is toss and turn, and wonder if our dreams are what we really want. It always happens at night. Then "Presto", day-light and a new day to try to get those dreams."

"I envy you Eric, you always know where you're going, you're patient and you're comfortable. You're kind too, because you eat all my crazy food and call it good," laughing, remembering his face as he tasted the squid.

"Now that your relaxed again, lets get some sleep. I teach an early class tomorrow. Can I have my arm back."

"Eric make love to me!"

Catching his breath, he was silent for awhile.

"Annie, I can't. I thank you for asking me, but I never was too good with one night stands. You will be leaving soon and I'll never see you again. I wish we could be lovers, but we're not right for each other. Annie, I care for you very much," then softly, "I don't want to fall in love with you again."

"O.K. professor, sorry I asked. I needed some loving tonight. Your a stick-in-a-mud."

"I know and you've got cold feet and you smell like garlic."

She giggled, pounded up her pillow and turned to the wall, remarking, "I snore too!"

Eric laid awake along time, feeling her body heat, listening to her breathing and letting his mind beat his heart back into his rib cage.

A week later Eric was home alone. He had finished up his paper work and turned in early.

At mid-night Annie came home all excited, she had landed the job in New York City, and had been celebrating with friends.

Wanting to tell Eric right then, she bounded into his bedroom. Leaped upon his bed, straddled his figure and yelled, "Eric I got the job, I got the job, wake up and listen."

"For crying out loud Annie, I'm awake. Stop yelling! You're sitting on my chest! You're drunk!"

"I know, we had some drinks to celebrate. Eric I got the news today. I can start this week and one of the girls has an apartment I can share, 'til I find something. Katy is going to take me to the airport and I'm ------."

"Hold it! Slow down! First get off my chest, so I can get enough air to form some words."

As he pulled himself to a sitting position against the head-board, she sat down on the edge of the bed. Lighting two cigarettes she gave him one.

"Oh Eric, my dreams have come true, at last. I made it."

Eric had just seen his beautiful whirl-i-gig in motion. So proud, so sure, so excited and so very lovely.

"Annie I knew you would make it. I'm proud of you. Congratulations Big Shot."

"Thanks and thank you for helping me through this period. I used you Eric, but I didn't have anyone else. Besides you don't stick your nose in my business."

"Now, I have a confession. I loved having you here. My apartment will be dreary after your gone. You make me enjoy life, Annie. I was taking from you too. I'll miss you my friend."

"Let me stay to-night Eric, and I'll give you a "going-away" present."

"That gift, would be a "Hello-I'm-giving-up-my-job-and-marrying-you-Eric", present."

"Your a macho monster."

"And you're drunk and on a high."

"Who cares?"

Turning at the doorway she said, "I hate your pajamas." He could hear her giggling across the hall.

Eric lit another cigarette and let his thoughts wander.

"At last the day had come. She would be gone. She had stirred memories alive, and made some new ones. She had never mentioned love. It was his fault for falling in love. He knew he would hate the man, that took the "spin" away from his precious whirl-i-gig."

HIRED MAN

Terry's barn-cat was draped across his shoulders, as he bent into his long strides and up-on-tip-toe gait, as he leisurely crossed the distance between the small farm house and dairy barn.

Clinging to a finger, the little hand barely closing together, was a skipping moppet, whom loved to be with her friend.

Looking down into two trusting eyes, he drawled, "As long as we have eaten, we better see to feeding the cows."

She looked up six feet into his face and nodded, not noticing it wasn't a face every one would consider handsome. A scraggly half bearded face, turned down bottom lip, eyes too close and over-all pocked-marked skin, topped off by a slicked-down-with-soap hair style.

Suzy knew she was going to sit on his lap and ride the tractor, he would put her on his shoulders and they would climb way up to the top of the silo, and Terry always let her help spread the hay, after he opened a bale.

As they walked, Terry's thoughts went through his mind like a computer read-out.

"I like this little tyke. She trusts me and loves me for I can make her laugh. She thanks me by throwing her little arms around my neck and kisses me. It makes up for the nights at the Village Bar, where women only stare or always make sure they are two stools away."

Looking at Suzy and spitting out hurtful words, he said, "I'm glad little friend, you don't know how ugly I am."

Evening chores finished, the two walking with a togetherness went back to the farm house.

Entering the big eat-in kitchen, Betty was doing up the dishes, turning she said, "Coffee pots still warm, might's well have a cup before you walk to the village, and Suzy you get those boots off."

"How do you know I'm going to the village?," as he hung his barn coat on a nail by the wood range.

"Today was check day and it's the week-end, and your off tomorrow morning, as Charlie took tonight off. Didn't have to be smart to figure that out," smiling as she wiped her hands.

Looking at Suzy she remarked, "It also looks like a spoiled brat is waiting for you to pull a couple of boots."

Terry looked at Suzy and she had one leg extended toward him smiling.

"She sure knows how to get her way," grinning at Betty and pulling at the same time.

"Charlie leave early today, Betty?"

"Yep, got to get down-street and plant crops, and breed heifers and brag with the boys."

Soon two more blond heads came around the corner and jumped into Terry's lap. While he was drinking his coffee, the youngster's slid down his long legs, as a slide, all the way to his size fourteen boots.

Betty sat down with her coffee and pulled the cross-word puzzle over to her.

Terry looked at her and thought, "God, what I wouldn't do for a wife like that."

At that moment he hated Charlie, knowing he was down at the Village Bar playing around. Hated Charlie that had everything he wanted, and never would have.

Silently he went into his room and changed his clothes.

As he reappeared in the kitchen, Betty looked up and with an impish grin said, "See you in the morning, Terry."

"Take a bet on that?"

"Yep."

"You'll lose to-night. Good-night kids, mind mama."

Getting the kids to bed, filling up the wood stove, and checking to see if the dog was out, was Betty's last chores for the evening. Now to get into those new books from the library.

Pulling up an easy chair and sticking her feet upon the oven door, was her position every night. Her books would take her all over the world, as she read 'til mid-night most nights.

Charlie wouldn't be back to bother her, and by then he would be too drunk to know where he was.

Eleven-thirty, just as she started to put her book up, the back door opened.

"Lost your bet, Betty."

"You must be sick."

"Nope, just not in the mood for women to-night. Only got a snoot-full."

As he pulled a chair up to the stove, she noticed a small bottle, he was holding.

"What's that, Terry."

"My medicine, that's what makes me want to get out of bed in the morning. I sit it down near the bed, and drink it before I get up."

"God Terry, I didn't know you were addicted."

"Yep, sure am. You never noticed, because I keep my beer in the milk cooler. It's all I'll ever have out of this life."

Looking at her, he wanted so much to reach out and take her foot in his hand and play "This little pig went to market" and make her laugh.

"Terry what's wrong, you are so sad to-night?"

"Well, I guess I'm lonesome. Since I've been a hired man on this place, I realize I want what Charlie has," and with sharp words, "What he don't give a damn about."

Betty looked down at her book, because the pain in his face was too private to look at.

"I'm sorry Betty - its the whiskey talking. I'm going to move on, in the morning. I'm getting too attached to you and the kids. I can't stand the way Charlie's gone every night, the way he's treating you."

"I guess Terry, you should have gone to Saratoga to-night and visited a women."

"That's what makes me sad. I know that's the only place, I'll ever hold a women, because as homely as I am, the only way is to buy it. I'm tired of being an out-cast. No real home, no wife, never any kids and buying love from someone, who hates it as much as I do. You treat me right-nice here and I love the kids. You never notice how homely I am. I've watched your face and your smile is real, like the kids.

So, I got to move on. I'll help with the chores in the morning. He'll need help. Good-night."

"Good-night Terry and thanks for sharing your thoughts."

Betty's wild evening of traveling around London in her books, had dropped to a sad ending, for she had felt all the pain in Terry's words. The first time she had ever seen him so sad, a terrifying sadness.

Breakfast was quieter than usual, except for the kids. Terry played with them, but not with his customary outbursts of laughter.

Charlie was sullen, so Betty knew Terry had told him, that today was his last. Never was too hard to get hired men, many had come and gone up 'till now.

About a month later, the trucker that hauled the milk cans, brought news of Terry.

As he was throwing milk cans upon his truck, he hollered above the noise of the milking machines.

"Guess what happened to Terry, your old hired-man?"

Charlie looked up, "What? Where did he go?"

"Living down by the river and last night, he pumped two bullets, into his chest. You know what? He was so drunk he never killed himself. He had a car and was sitting in it and when he realized he wasn't going to die, he drove himself to the hospital. Can't imagine why he did it. The only time anyone shoots their self is over a woman. I don't think he got too enthusiastic over those in Saratoga, and I know they wouldn't fight over that homely old codger."

"I'll be damn," said Charlie.

"So he's alright then," Betty said quietly.

Betty walked to the open barn door and gazed out over the fields.

"His last performance and he couldn't get what he wanted. Another failure to live with. He couldn't even shut out the laughter, that all his life, he had, had to listen to, as people made jokes about him.

All he wanted was to have someone to care."

She sighed, and whispered softly, "I'm sorry Terry."

Turning she picked up a pitch-fork and started spreading out the hay in front of the cows.

DARK DARKNESS

The middle-age Lady, well kept and sophisticated sat at a corner table, listening to the sounds of the Hotel Dinning Room.

Always the same, day after day. Living here, gave her a stable freedom of movements as she was totally blind.

Gwyn was admired for her grace and outer poise, but inside grew a dark, revengeful, cankerous sore.

Ten years ago it happened.

She hated in silence.

Gwyn's brooding mind played the scene over and over again, the last fight between her and her husband, Don. She had loved him in spite of his uncontrollable temper.

Their apartment air was full of angry, loud, hurtful words and reflected the hot blazing eyes as they tormented each other.

Turning her back on him, she went into the bath and stood looking in the mirror.

The old iron door-stopper, just missing her head, imbedded it's self in the mirror. Sending millions of fine splinters of glass into her face. At the same time Don slammed the door for the last time.

Grabbing her face, she screamed, for her hands had pushed the long protruding splinters deeper into her flesh.

Unable to open her eyes, she staggered to the next apartment and was rushed to the hospital.

To exist, Gwyn had arrange her life around her open sightless eyes.

Don paid the bills, but never spoke to her again.

As her mind was wandering, she heard foot-steps approaching her table, then stop by it.

"Gwyn."

Recognizing Don's voice, she started to shake and dropped her hands into her lap, where the nails dug, piercing her palms.

"Please may I sit down, I need to talk to you?"

Forcing herself to speak, she said, "It's been a long time, so what's the need now? Sit if you wish."

"Gwyn for ten years, I haven't been able to live with myself. I've hated myself for blinding you and leaving like a coward. I knew you hated me and I was too weak to face your torment, also your wrath. I come to see how you were and would like to help, other then just pay the bills."

Gwyn thought, "So now he wants to be relieved of his guilt. He can't live with his guilt, but I have to live with my darkness."

The sore inside started to burn and a plan formed.

"Would you like to see the apartment you have provided for me all these years and where we can discuss our plight in private?"

Taking his arm, they walk to the elevator.

"Don, as much as I hated you, I must admit it seems nice to feel a man's arm again," Gwyn said sweetly.

Entering the apartment, Don noticed many things he had given her, that she still kept.

"I'm surprised you haven't thrown away all those little things that would remind you of me."

"Reminders have been the fire that has kept me going."

"You have done well, Gwyn. Your just as beautiful and well dressed as always."

"I have something special to show you. Stand right where you are."

Going into the bedroom, Gwyn removed a forty-five pistol from a drawer and held it behind her.

Walking up behind him, she placed one hand on his shoulder, placed the gun at the base of his skull and pulled the trigger.

Don slowly slumped to the floor.

Hearing the loud report, a maid opened the door, looked and went screaming to the office.

The detective took the gun from her hand and lead her to the door.

"Are his eyes open?" she asked.

"Yes ma'am!"

"Now I have left him staring into the solid black darkness!"

A TURTLE SLED

It had been snowing during the night, but in the morning the sun was shining making the meadow glisten.

Over under a big pine tree, the snow was moving, soon it was flying in all directions. When the snow stopped flying, out hopped a Rabbit, just as white as the snow.

The Rabbit sat there looking around. None of his little animal friends was out playing in the snow.

After awhile he felt lonesome, so he decided he would go looking for someone to talk to.

Down at the bottom of the hill was a pond, where his friend the turtle and frog lived. So hopping and jumping in and out of the snow, he hurried down to the pond.

It was a warm day, so no ice had formed on the water. The Rabbit knew that Turtle was sleeping, just under the mud near the bank.

Sticking his paws down into the mud, he found Turtle, and scooped him up and laid him on the bank.

Turtle was still half asleep and he hollered at Rabbit, "What the heck are you doing? You know I like to sleep late!"

"I'm lonesome and I want someone to play in the snow with me," said Rabbit.

"Play in the snow.? I can't play in the snow, my legs are too short."

"We could slide down hill," pleaded Rabbit.

"Slide down hill! I just told you I can't walk in this deep snow. Don't you listen? I couldn't get up the hill to slide down."

"Sure you could Turtle. I could pull you up the hill by your tail."

"And pray what would we slide down hill on? You don't own a sled!"

"We could use your shell as a sled. You could turn on your back, and I could sit on top of your shell and away down the hill we would go."

Turtle liked that idea, because he was a little lazy and he wouldn't have to do any walking. Going up hill for him was hard work, and he couldn't walk fast.

"Alright Rabbit, let's slide down hill."

Rabbit was so happy he grabbed the Turtle's tail and started hopping up the hill. He hopped so fast, the Turtle was bouncing up and down, also flipping this way and that. All the flippity-floppity made the turtle dizzy.

"Hey, slow down Rabbit. Your banging me so hard I'm getting a headache."

"I'm sorry Turtle," said Rabbit as he slowed down.

Sitting on top of the hill, Rabbit and Turtle looked at each other and laughed.

"This is going to be lots of fun, you wait and see Turtle."

Turning Turtle over on his back, Rabbit put his front paws onto the shell and pushed with his strong back legs. After getting the shell moving fast, Rabbit hopped upon the shell and sat down.

They flew down hill so fast, Rabbit had to bend his ears downward, because the wind made a whistling sound in them.

When they got to the bottom, they laughed and rolled in the snow, because it was so much fun sliding down hill.

"Let's do it again, Turtle. Did you like it!"

"Wow, that was fun, Rabbit. Yea, let's do it again. But this time, let me go down backward. The snow keeps coming in all over my head and I can't see."

So Rabbit placed the turtle backward and he pushed off, then reached down grabbed Turtle's tail and stood up.

"Gosh! This is just like surf-boarding on the water," Rabbit squealed.

They went up and down a few more times and soon Rabbit was standing on one leg and going down hill like an acrobat.

Turtle said, "I've got to go home."

"Just once more, please?" begged Rabbit.

"Alright once more."

As this was going to be the last time, Rabbit decided he would give a good, hard push, so they could go farther and have a longer ride.

Getting to the top of the hill, Rabbit turned Turtle over. Rabbit grabbed the shell and ran as hard as he could before jumping on. He grabbed Turtle's tail and stood up on one leg, with the other leg way out in back of him.

How fast they sailed down the hill. Rabbit felt like a circus performer riding bareback on a horse.

All of a sudden the turtle sled hit a rock, and Rabbit went flying through the air. His body turned over and over, with his big ears flopping all over.

He was going so fast through the air, that he landed in the pond, with a big splash. The splash made so much noise, it woke up all the sleeping fish and frogs.

Sticking their heads out of the mud, they started hollering.

"What do you think your doing Rabbit? All you do is go around disturbing your friends. Why can't you be quiet?"

Poor Rabbit, he was all wet and all his friends were hollering at him.

He looked around for Turtle. There was Turtle just coming up to the bank of the pond.

"Are you all right Turtle?"

"Yes, I'm all right Rabbit. It looks like I have to help you out of the water. Grab my tail and I'll pull you out, like a motorboat. I have a chip in my shell, where we hit that rick."

"I'm sorry Turtle."

Getting Rabbit to shore was not easy, because Rabbit was heavy to pull.

As Rabbit crawled upon the bank he said, "I had a nice time today. I'm glad you slid down hill with me. I'm all wet now, so I have to hurry home and get warm and dry."

"See you tomorrow Rabbit," said Turtle as he crawled back in the pond, under the mud.

Rabbit was feeling cold, so he hopped as fast as he could to his hole under the pine tree.

He snuggled down into his bed and soon was fast asleep, dreaming of his turtle sled.

THE "DAWN"

The evening ocean was silently pushing the quiet waves up over the sand.

Every night, I strolled along the waters edge, relaxing, making peace with myself before seductive sleep caught me unaware.

The Wading-in-the-surf distant figure completed my walk, for she was a dear friend, and every year vacationer. I wondered why I hadn't seen Monique this summer. She usually came before the last week. I had lots to tell her about things that had happened in N.Y.C., last winter.

Catching up with me we set our stride. We knew each other so well, we had no desire to talk, casting our own spell, which was comfortable. We always took these evening walks together. The winding down of the day.

I tipped my head to glance at her, and her face burst into a smiling glory all her own, which I had seen many times.

Turning my head, to glance at the sea, I was troubled by an extra spark in her eye, I thought I had seen, only fleetingly. Something was different about her tonight.

Several steps further, her hand crept into mine, which she never ventured before.

Caressingly her thumb moved over my fingers, the movements taking the form of love being expressed.

Instantly that made excitement race thru my body, which startled me. She was my friend, why did she now play the part of a lover, putting on the "make"?

I stopped walking, our eyes met, soaking up feelings, so powerful, there was no mistake, she was telling me, she loved me. I was thunder struck, we had never had thoughts of love.

Looking at Monique tonight I realized, she was very beautiful. I knew we would make love tonight, by the sea, and it was an exciting thought.

Walking, thoughtfully, we headed for her cottage.

Taking my hand she led me to the sofa, saying, "Sit down, there is something I have to explain to you."

Pushing me down, she knelt in front of me laying her head upon my knees, and caressing my thighs.

"Remember last year, when I had a broken heart and you held me and consoled me?"

"Yes," I said.

"That's when it started, my falling in love with you. Having been friends for so long, I was surprised, my feelings took this kind of a turn. I came out here this year once more, to make love with you. I shall not come again, for I am going to get married."

I couldn't believe my life-long summer friend would not be sharing my life by the sea any longer, and I knew this year would be my last also, for her absences would make the sea cold and dull the excitement.

She reached up in under my shirt and caressed my stomach.

"Your skin is like velvet! Do you know where we will make love? Out on the deck that is covered with sleeping bags. That way we can watch the stars and feel the cool breeze on our bodies."

"I never realized you were such a tease before," and I reached out to lay my hands along side of her face, but she quickly slid away.

"Oh! No! You are not touching me yet, because I will give in and make love, right here in the living room, and I want this to be special tonight."

I followed her over to the sliding glass doors, which lead to the deck. Holding hands we gazed at the moon and sea. I couldn't believe this was our last night.

"Put on your Bikini and stand over by the railing, with the moon at your back, and watch for me to come thru the deck doors."

I had positioned myself exactly as she wanted and wondered what she was up to now. Here was a girl I had known all my life, we were such sharing friends, and now, with a twist of fate, we had become lovers.

A shimmering, satiny figure had appeared and stood still for a fleeting moment, before floating towards me, on rippling muscled legs, with hips swaying, like a Lioness approaching her prey.

Her short stylish night-wear caught the light, making me catch my breath and my groin knot up. She was so beautiful.

Coming towards me she raised her arms, wrapping them around my neck, and laid her body against mine, which made me ache.

"Don't touch me, let me stay against you and kiss me on the shoulders."

"I love you," escaped from my lips.

"I have been waiting a whole year to hear you say that," and she laid her head on my chest contented.

I enfolded her in my arms, and I could have held her like that all night.

Walking with her, over to the spread out sleeping bags, we laid down on our backs and gazed sky-ward. They were the same old stars we had studied before, but now they seem to be a little bit sad, for they were going to miss her too.

She stretched her tanned leg over mine and laid her arm across my waist.

It was so comfortable having her near, I decided not to make a first move and spoil our last night.

Slipping out of her shimmering night-wear, she dropped it over my face and when I was able to see again, there she laid in her well tanned body. I had never seen her exposed before and feasted my eyes the whole length of her. As my eyes traveled to her face, she was smiling impishly.

"Do you like me?"

"I never saw such beauty, before. I've got to touch you, before you fade away in the moon light!"

She laughed, and took my hand and laid it just inside her thigh.

"Don't move one little finger, O.K?"

"If you think I am going to risk losing this beautiful body, your crazy. Your one damn sexy girl!"

Removing my hand from her thigh, I rolled over on my elbow and gazed down into her face. My finger traced her eye brows and the outline of her lips. Wanting desperately to kiss her I dipped my head, but just as quickly she covered my lips with her hand.

"I am not teasing you," she said, "I know that if we make too much contact, it will be all over for me. I want to stay with you until dawn, and I want to spend the better part of the evening being blissfully content. When I'm with you I'm always at peace."

"I never realized," I said, "why I put such energy into trying to have a vacation out here. Now that you say you will never be coming back, I know also, that you were the reason I came every year. I also was at peace with you, even helping you solve your bigger than life problems, that weren't."

"All my problems were big!"

"And now, you are adding to them, by making love to me. Are you sure you won't have a hang up afterwards."

"No! making love with a person as beautiful and gentle as you are, should give me a memory, to stabilize me whenever I wish to remember it. Let me have this night with no scolding's. Please."

"You know, I could never scold, except when you might do some harm to your self. You my impetuous lovely, can always seem, to get into a fix without trying. But tonight I approve of your escapade, so let the chips fall where they may."

"I am glad, your glad," and she rolled over showing her back to me.

"What's this a cold shoulder so soon?"

"No! lets play chairs. Slide over and fit your body next to mine. Now I am sitting in your lap."

"If we stay like this too long, I'm going to have to jump into the sea. Have you ever seen a sea boil?"

She laughed.

"And now my Lady Godiva what do you suggest I do with my arm, that seems to be hanging in space?"

She reached back took my wrist and pulled my arm across her middle and then tucked by hand between her rib skin and the sleeping bag.

"You know walking across the deck toward me, I thought you were the essence of loveliness, but feeling your bony rib, I guess I let the stars get in my eyes."

"Ribs are lovely, that's why Eve was made from one. Stop thinking of bones and think of all the love that's hiding under that rib, inside my heart. I love you so much!"

Lying content with her, I thought about my Diary, I had kept every summer. I didn't know it then, but I had wanted to keep her alive and with me all winter.

Lazily she asked, "Are you going to put this in your diary?"

"Your psychic, I was just thinking of my diary. No, this is too special to be written down by one person. It is being shared by two this night, and so my Diary died. When you get back to your business, "Exotic Fashions" and start putting together your new line and fashion shows, you will never remember this night. Your little five foot frame has an energy that propels you and with your new designer, you both will be caught up in your other life."

"You also. Your big, proud, successful Publishing House in Manhattan, also makes you into a different person. We couldn't have more of each other, for with me in Paris and you over here, I guess we would have to meet at Airports."

"We are two successful people, that have used up our vacation time at last. Also a little slow learning what is important about loving a person."

I looked up at the full moon and looked down upon the still, relaxed, naked body I was holding. I raised to my knees, both arms extended to the moon and pleaded to Diana, "the Moon Goddess."

"Diana, you lovely lady that the Greeks made into a God. Now, look at us! I have a beautiful person here, that I know is as lovely as you were. You look upon her face and Bless her over the years and please let me know if she ever needs me. I shall always love, and worship both of you."

My nymph by the sea, rolled over onto her stomach and hid her face. I asked what was the matter, and she looked up and said, "Loving a person like you, is wonderful. You make me feel so important, so loved and I swear I am beginning to feel like the most beautiful girl in the world."

"You won't make first place, because you have a mole on the back of your Butt."

Well she fairly tied her self into a knot trying to find that mole.

She saw me smiling and stopped all gyrations, rolled over and put her head on my stomach, saying, "I love you! Why does it seem to be the only words we can say?"

"Because those three little words, hold all the emotion that people feel. They can make you, or break you. They should never be used unless backed up by a heartful of real love."

I let my hand lightly and slowly caress her body, I felt her muscles respond and tighten when the caress was pleasurable. I dropped my hand to cover her breast and already her nipple was hard. I commanded my hand to lie still on the sleeping bag. I knew the night was too young and I wanted peace as long as she did.

I gently put her head on the sleeping bags, so I could stand up. Quickly grabbing my ankle she said, "Please don't go. Are you mad?"

Laughing I stood up, "Haven't you heard that at all the great feasts, they serve wine. I am now going to raid your wine rack."

Returning with a tray of wine, cheeses, glasses and napkins, I sat it on deck and we sat cross-legged facing each other.

I raised my glass.

"As I drink this wine, I'm toasting you with every sip, so shall I remember you, where-ever I shall drink wine again. I am glad you made me realize I loved you more than a friend. This night should be sad, but it is excitable and peaceful, both together.

Your life with me is not over for I care about you. You are free to walk into my life anytime and you are free to bring me your problems."

"You will be so jealous, you'll hate me when we spilt in the morning."

"Being human, yes, I will be jealous, that only means I still love you, hate you, never. This night brings two friends together in a bond of love. This kind of love, can never breed hate. If I hadn't felt something special for you, just putting that "make" on me wouldn't have worked."

"You have so many ways of telling me you love me and I know you do. I have been a friend, too many years, not to know the type of person you are. You are gentle and kind, and not a liar, and you talk too much."

"Come over on this side of the tray and give me a sensuous kiss, that will keep my mouth closed."

Looking me straight in the eye, she slowly unfolded her crossed legs, stood up and walked toward me.

Tipping me backward and down flat on my back she pinned my arms along side of my body, with her knees and commenced a long sensuous kiss, sitting on my stomach.

Her lips turned me to fire and the hot little body sitting on my stomach was branding me with the word love.

My God! I had to do something, so I flipped her over putting her on bottom and gently drawing her full length against me, continued kissing passionately.

I knew we had continued too long, when she started making begging, pleading noises. We were both so keyed up we almost ruined our night.

I quickly rolled off, pulled my mouth from hers and gathered her into my arms just holding her, so she would relax.

She was exciting to make love to and I knew, it would be beautiful later on.

We laid still and at peace. I thought about us. Two kids from rich families, that owned Beach Cottages, and our families were friends, so we were always together every summer, all our lives. I remember when we were seven and eight year olds, she said I had to do what she wanted me to, because her Daddy made more money than mine. I wasn't taking that lying down, so I asked my Mom if we were richer then they were. Mom said both families had the same amount of money. Well that shot her Ace-in-the-hole. She never bossed me around again, unless I concede she is bossing me around tonight.

She always was special to me, because she loved life and was ready for anything that came into her head to do. She put sparkle into my life, but loving her, I couldn't believe it. I knew that being friends was all we could have and never thought about getting involved any deeper.

Now our last time at the Beach was over-whelming us. Like her, I knew this memory would always be with me, only mine would always be making me look for her in any crowded place.

The body I held, was still for so long, I thought she had fallen asleep. The thought had no more then flitted thru my head, when she whispered, "Let go of me you sex maniac!"

"I am sorry, not for kissing you like that, but because I lost my head and didn't want to stop. You stoked my furnace too hard and I forgot my promise, until I heard you groan. I knew then, I had taken advantage of you and I felt like I had betrayed you. But, By God! making love to you is pure joy."

She lifted her head off my chest, and was starting to move away, but I caught her by the chin and planted a kiss between her brows.

She sat up and looked me square in the eye and said, "Nobody's ever kissed me like that before, or if they have, I wasn't in love with them, because it was the first time I couldn't stop myself. Also that tender kiss on my forehead was born out of really caring for me. Go-to-bed partners never bother being tender, just get down to business time.

Damn, I wish we could be together more, but my fashion's wouldn't sell here as well and your publishing house, needs it's contacts here. We are caught in a web, in more ways than one."

"Unless we still want to use our Beach Homes for holidays or summer. You could post me a letter and I would come. That is if you don't marry. When you marry, I will have no deceit going on. We are both too well-known and would surely make a slip sometime.

I shall never marry, I have no need for it. If I need sex, I can always hire the services and get exactly what I want. You my love, is the only human in the world, that can ever make me come running."

"There you go running off at the mouth again."

"Want to quiet it again, like the last time?"

"No, I'm going to stuff it with wine and cheese."

"Well, poor me I knew this would be my unlucky night."

She quickly stood up and went to pour some more wine. Watching her, she could have made a pretty picture for some wine ad. Her tan naked body showing thru the white wine bottle, she held in one hand, and holding two wine glasses in the other, hoping to fill both of them, while she is flirting with me.

"Lets sit back to back while we sip, and listen to the night sounds."

"O.K!" I said, "Just as long as your boney spine doesn't leave black and blue marks."

"Poor sport, mad cause you can't have your own way. I would get along swell with-out you, if I could, but I can't and I don't want to."

"Well, if you listen to me complain, I guess I'll have to continue to listen to your crack-pot ideas. A love-in with no love."

"Yes, there is love, more than we can ever use up."

It was quiet, the waves gently caressing the beach, the moon starting toward its morning waning. The red flickering of a late night beach fire, farther up the coast.

A cozy warm setting to lie down beside each other and let our skin touch. We both sat our wine glasses down at the same time, turned, and she said, "Let's lie together touching."

"My God, we even think alike."

I laid down and put my arm out and she put her head on my shoulder and pulled my arm around her. She put her arm around my waist.

Soon her hand was caressing my skin, from my breast to my pelvic.

Such light strokes, putting pressure in certain areas, stopping her hand, long enough for my body to scream "please go on".

She must have caught my breathing because she whispered, "You like me loving your skin, and I love feeling it."

"Yes, I love it and you have the gift for making my skin cry out. My turn to caress you now!"

She turned on her back and I leaned my head on her shoulder. The smell of her skin was clean, and very enjoyable. My hand traced her body, following every dip, becoming more demanding by putting pressure to her erotic zones. Feeling skin is very hypnotizing. Slowly my hand moved without thinking and I was holding her breast, I knew I wouldn't let go this time and I knew I was going to slip my mouth right down on top of it.

I let my hand stray down to her pelvic gridle and rest inside of her thigh.

I turned my body onto my stomach and was kissing her breast, letting my tongue play with her hard nipple. I slowly moved my hand up from her thigh and covered her pubic hair, and just let it lie still. Her passionate body was trying to hold back, but her hips were slowly catching on fire. I knew this time she was mine.

I was beginning to feel the excitement and I put my hand way down her leg, and slowly drew it up on the inside, nearing her thighs, she released her leg tension, giving me permission to enter her. I covered her with my whole hand, and drew one finger along her vagina.

I groaned the same time she did for finding her lubricated and ready, I wanted her now.

I was taking no chances she would cool and make me stop. So I cradled her hips and gently, but demandingly kissed her stomach and thighs.

After a few minutes she was like an over-wound mechanical toy.

She brought to me so much excitement, I lost my head too.

The stars watched two lovers soak up a life time of held back love, but doing it so gently, tenderly and thinking of each others welfare.

As she lay spent beside me, I put her head on my shoulder enfolded her in my arms and let her know, I loved her. I also whispered, "Thanks".

We laid there until Mr. Sun started to push Mr. Darkness away. Also was telling Mr. Fog to follow Mr. Darkness, they never argued with Mr. Sun.

With tears in her eyes, she stirred and rose up to a sitting position. Looking into my eyes, she said, "I now know the difference between love and sex. I also know I love you and always will. Our chemistry is perfect and this was the first time I ever got to cloud nine. I shall never get married now. I couldn't, you can't make a go of something you can't feel. If you still want me I will send a card different Holidays, saying where I'll be. To me this was not our last night, forever. It was our starting of a forever, last night. I love you, my gentle friend and lover."

As she turned to face the sun rise, I dressed. Coming back out on the deck I looked at her lovely, quiet body leaning on the rail and again her vision caused me to gasped.

"Will you come inside and kiss me good-by, until next time?"

"No, my love! Because I would tease you to stay and you would if I asked. I have to get use to leaving you. I want to start now, while I can. When you get down the beach don't look back, or wave because my tears will be filling my eyes, and mixing with the sand below. That makes us part of this earth. Every night I will look at the moon and remember you begging Diana to watch over me, and I'll be whispering your name, hoping the breezes, carries my words to New York.

I love you and, " - there the words broke and she bowed her head.

"I love you very much, my love. Remember the wine, our everlasting toast. We both are sad but we shed tears of happiness, knowing we belong to each other forever."

Turning I stumbled down the stairs to the beach below, walking far enough away I stopped, the urge to turn and look back was over-powering. Instead I bent and wrote her name in the sand and after wrote mine. Then traced over again the words,

MONIQUE and PAGE - BEACH LOVERS.

LADY FOREVER

Walking into my apartment, after a morning of shopping, I threw my packages onto the sofa, switched on my Call Girl answering service, on the way to the kitchen.

I would write down my appointments while sipping a cocktail.

Good there was only one, for tonight. I liked that trick, it was a night where I would be treated like a rich lady, that was loved and adored.

Staring out the window with my drink in my hand, I remembered the first time I was called to work for him. Very handsome, shy, seventy-one year old man. He wanted nothing but the company of a beautiful lady, to eat supper with him. He treated me fine for he was of the old time rich, Park Avenue homes.

Mr. D. had lost his wife, which he adored very much and about once a week he would like to entertain a lady like he did his loved one.

The Agency had sent me the first time he had called. They knew I had come from a rich home, had a good private University degree, and had class.

I was glad I got to go, because he was good for me, as much as I was good for him.

My family was rich once and then Wall Street let us down, so by the necessity of making a living I was use to, I became an expensive Call Girl.

The first night his housekeeper met me at the door and explained everything that Mr. D. would expect of me, for the evening. Her and I grew to respect each other and together tried to make Mr. D. happy.

The only trick that was without sex, this let me relax. It was the only appointment, where I was treated with respect.

After showering and pampering my body, I slipped into a black, lowcut, with sexy folds and sides slit, soft as silk dress. Just before going out the door I took one last look in the full mirror.

I smiled, winked and said, "Good-luck Lady D., this is one night you'll come home, looking as good as you left."

Swinging thru the apartment doors, I spotted Mr. D's. limo waiting. The chauffer helped me in, and from there on in I was Lady D.

The housekeeper answered my door ring, and greeted me smiling.

"Mr. D's., in the library waiting to serve you cocktails."

"Thank you, Maggie."

Stepping into the library, I saw Mr. D. mixing our drinks. He turned smiled and holding out a cocktail toward me, said, "I am glad you came. I like your company. My! you look very beautiful tonight."

The only man that called me beautiful. The others always said, "sexy".

He motioned we sit on the white sofa, near the French doors, which looked out over New York City.

I was so content looking at all the lights with Mr. D. holding my hand and kissing it every once in a while.

Soon Maggie announced supper, which was a lovers setting. Soft candle light reflected off the crystal.

The table was different tonight, so much more elegant than ever before.

"Lady D. tonight is special, I am going to make a request of you. You may say no if you like. We've known each other a long time now. You have made me very happy eating supper with me and spending evenings in my company. I have grown to care for you very much. Your career is your own business, and I wouldn't have met you at all if not for the Agency.

Tonight is different because I want you to spend the night with me. Not because you are getting paid. I'm old and I would like once more to lie beside of a beautiful women. I would feel honored."

I couldn't believe my ears, this man was asking me if I would mind, when all he had to do was tell me, for he was paying the bill. He was gently telling me he cared about me.

Looking him straight in the eye, I said, "Mr. D., I would love to have you go to bed with me. It's a nice feeling to have someone really care for you."

He smiled, relaxed and actually blushed.

"I shopped today for you, hoping you would spend the night. When supper is over Maggie will show you your gifts. Also I have a special gift for you now, I hope you except it, for it was bought to adorn you and is given with lots of affection."

Rising he walked over behind me carrying a box. Handing me the box he said softly, "Open it."

It was the most beautiful emerald and diamond necklace I had ever seen. So delicate.

"It's too rich for me, Mr. D. It belongs on a Queen, not me. I couldn't accept this."

Yet my heart was aching to wear it.

He took it, settled it around my neck, stood back and looked at me.

"To me you are a Queen, the necklace is beautiful on you and your beauty makes it more beautiful. It is a gift for you, for filling my lonely hours with pleasure, and always being a lady. You have been able to give me contentment and this is the only way I can do anything for you. Wear it with all my blessings."

He saw the tears in my eyes and bent over and kissed my cheek.

"Be happy, not sad, Lady D."

Everything was perfect, the delicious supper, the gift of love, the evening with beautiful music, and lovely talk.

At nine o'clock Maggie entered and said she would show me to my room.

For the first time I entered Mr. D's bedroom. So masculine and elegant.

Lying on the bed were many boxes.

"These are the gifts Mr. D. bought for you today. They are yours to keep. He was very nervous about tonight, but he has a special place in his heart for you. He doesn't look upon you as a paid Call Girl. I think he really and truly worships you. He is concerned about your future and what will happen to you. He has become very protective of you, you are his Queen."

Opening the boxes, I was so thrilled.

"Oh! Maggie, such a beautiful negligé."

Opening another box, I cried, real tears.

"Maggie a real Sable coat. My God! it's out of this world. How can I except these gifts?"

"You must Lady D.! He would be heart-broken if you don't. He wants only to make you happy. You are the substitute for his beloved wife. It gives him something to live for again. I will leave you now, Mr. D. will be in shortly."

164

I was standing in front of the mirror wearing the coat when thru the open door Mr. D. appeared.

I turned to face him and he had a smile from ear to ear.

"I knew you would look like that in it."

"You are the kindest man, I have ever met. You know my trade yet spoil me rotten. Let me say now, I have enjoyed all our evenings together. I have never felt paid for. You have given me pride in my self, by making me important, by treating me like a lady, and liking my company for myself. You don't need to buy me gifts, you have already given me so much more. You have never made me feel cheap, you are a kind, gentle and caring person."

Walking towards him I put my arms around his neck for the first time, and kissed him gently.

Then teasingly I said, "Now, I shall model my beautiful negligée."

"Please do," he said and sat down in an easy chair.

I knew this night I wouldn't be parading around the room like a stripper, I would do it modestly as a wife would undress. He watched every movement I made until I was clothed in my elegant negligée.

He asked me to sit at the dressing table and brush my hair for him. Standing behind me he just stared into the mirror before he said, "Your beautiful -". Then he choked up.

Turning out the lights, he led me to the bed. Putting my head on his shoulder he hugged me with both arms.

I put my hand on his chest and let it slowly drift, caressing him.

"You don't have to love me," he said, "I just want to hold you."

"Shush! I want to," I whispered.

I knew I was experienced and I was going to make this friend of mine have the best evening ever, because I wanted it this way.

Removing my negligée, I laid my body as close to his as I could get and started removing his pajamas.

Lying quietly with our bodies touching was slowly making him respond.

As I rolled over and kissed him passionately but gently, all the forgotten fire of his body responded and it became a night for lovers.

A couple of weeks later, Maggie called, "Lady D., Mr. D. passed away and you will be getting a letter written by him before he died. Do as exactly as he tells you. It's his last gift.

Lady D., I will miss you. Thanks for making him happy."

Opening the letter a few days later, it read, "Lady D., because I respected you and you made me feel important again, I want to make the rest of your life, so respectable you can live like the beautiful Lady which you are. I have settled enough money on you, so you will never, have to do anything you don't want to. My lawyer will contact you! Be happy and always be you, my understanding beautiful lady.

I adored you.

Mr. D."

Tears filled my eyes and I wept for a man that had made me a lady.

GRAM IN THE PARK

Did you ever play baseball with a three year old?

Do you realize how many miles you travel, throwing the ball, then chasing the ball, as he swings like a diseased manikin and stands there like the Statue of Liberty.

Of course sometimes he isn't even watching you, like he's real interested.

By this time your heart is giving your legs a "pep-rally" cheer.

Wondering what game you can play, just so you can sit down, you spy the swings.

Let me tell you, nothing you do with a three year old is easy, even sitting. If I had known that, I would have trotted the kid off home.

Now picture this, you are holding him on your lap, which slants at a 90° angle, both arms around the chains and around him, hoping he doesn't slide off your lap, trying to pump with your legs and all he wants to do is lean forward and stare at the ground.

His next big adventure is to throw his ball into a tall, rain-soaked, coke-left-over, garbage barrel, which has to be tipped over, as no one's arms grow that long.

The beautiful white ball now lies in this brown sticky, oil filmed puddle, and while Gram is deciding the best way to recapture the ball, this Einstein kid, moves swiftly. Of course he's fast, he hasn't done anything all day, but stand still and sit, while I've felt like I just completed the "Bataan Death March".

Getting the ball was no trouble for "swiftly", unless you abhor newly dyed-brown, white sneakers.

Did you ever notice they break the Hundred-yard dash Record, when doing something you don't want them to and put on their best arthritic walk, when you want them to hurry?

Now the big moment of the day, conquering the slide.

This nice, worrying, hope he don't fall, caring Gram, climbs the ladder behind this confident - Mountain climber, holding his jacket, when all motion stops half-way up and he turns and yells, "No Gram" and yanks the jacket out of your caring fingers.

Now you're so hurt, that he doesn't care, cause you care, you walk around to the bottom of the slide and hope he comes so fast, you can't catch him.

Well, you look up at this beaming little face and say, "Ready".

He says, "Ready" and let's go.

As he hits your arms, it's like you are Superman stopping Amtrak Express.

You wonder, if your arms are out of the socket or did they always hang loose like that, at your side.

You know it doesn't take a Master's Degree to be a Grandmother, just "Geratal".

All in all, we had what Grams are supposed to call fun.

MY ANCESTORS?

I sit and look at the big thick book, of traced back ancestors, and wonder why, it has become a must, proudly claimed thing to do.

We scurry patiently to the Town Historians, County Census Books, old decaying, moldy grave markers, and write heaping pages, of Dates and Names.

We're happily ecstatic, when we find them across the great ocean, in some other, not so nice Glorified European land.

Fleetingly, my History Class, slides across my mind, and I remember tiny bits and pieces of the far-off lands. Just because the English, of long ago left the British Isles, were they English?

Once war-like Rome trampled all the Countries of Europe, and later, Britain had many military possessions, on two continents. Way before that history, crude, warring Norsemen Vikings captured and raped.

And now, in case your pencil is still writing Dates and Names, journey back in time, to our real beginners.

"Paranthropus" gave in to "Australopithecus. They were replaced by "Homo-Erectus", which were trampled by "Neanderthal", who we think disappeared, before "Cro-Magnon Man".

I think its really like trying to catch, a fleeing fly, to figure out your elusive "genes", and changing nationality.

It looks like we are truly, only Homo-sapiens, and are the nationality of what ever country, we were born in.

Nobody wants to be totally American! What are they really looking for?

Our gutsy Ancestors willingly gave up their born in Country, to become Americans, and generations later, we want desperately to be attached to the very Country, they left in much disgust.

As my old Irish, I think, Ancestor once said, "John, you took me from Ireland to England, and I didn't want to go. I went later, from England to America, and I didn't want to go. Right now, this is the best of the lot, and I wouldn't go back to either one, if the spit of me mouth would take me there".

AUTHOR BIOGRAPHY

Anna grew up in upstate New York during the depression.

After graduation from high school she went to work for the phone company as a operator.

She married a young farmer, where they raised their 4 children on a dairy farm.

After a divorce she moved and went to work for the New York State where she retired from.

Her later years were spent enjoying her family and friends, in till her passing.

Printed in the United States
By Bookmasters